RELATIONAL
HOLINESS

Relational Holiness is a work as helpful as it is insightful. Oord and Lodahl help us bridge the credibility gap that has plagued the Holiness Movement from its inception. With a wonderful blend of biblical scholarship, theological insight, and pragmatic instruction, this book will help the reader understand that truly "there is no holiness but social (relational) holiness." This will be an important book for pastors, laypeople, and students who long to be holy as our Heavenly Father is holy.

—T. Scott Daniels
Pastor, Richardson Church of the Nazarene, Richardson, Texas

Professors Oord and Lodahl are representative of a number of younger theologians who are deeply committed to the Wesleyan-Holiness message but are theologically responsible in seeking to articulate the message in biblically sound ways that are relevant to the contemporary culture. They have grounded the core of the Holiness message, which they rightly see to be love, in the Trinitarian nature of God and, like the New Testament, elaborate its embodiment as being in the social context of the Christian community. This approach challenges the individualistic motif characteristic of Western culture since the Enlightenment, a motif that informed much earlier theologizing about sanctification in human experience. This book calls us to a biblically grounded, theologically responsible, livable life of holiness.

—H. Ray Dunning
Professor Emeritus of Theology, Trevecca Nazarene University, Nashville

University professors Thomas Oord and Michael Lodahl have written a primer to attract a new generation of seekers to the Holiness message. In *Relational Holiness* they have attempted to replace what they consider caricatures of the Holiness message with the true Holiness characteristic—love.

—Tom Nees
Director, USA/Canada Mission/Evangelism Department, Church of the Nazarene

Redeemed and holy existence is a life of dancing with the triune God according to the authors. And I agree. God is always lovingly responsive to us and like a dancer leaps into the air and lands again in perfect balance alongside us. God's responsiveness to our moves and steps fosters vitality and spontaneity in our lives.

The authors see that God exists in continuous and living relation to our decisions, desires, and needs. And God deals with us with freshness and creativity, ever moving us in the best directions but without violating our own integrity at all. The book should inspire many to take up God's serious call anew.

—Clark H. Pinnock
McMaster Divinity College, Hamilton, Ontario

Relational Holiness is an excellent resource for those committed to understanding and promoting the doctrine of holiness in the 21st century. Focusing on the core value of love, the authors draw on theological themes emphasized by John Wesley. They integrate other concepts of holiness within the theology of holiness understood as relational love. Engaging discussion questions promote the authors' goal of considering holiness in a social rather than just an individual context. Must reading for anyone—lay and clergy, student and professor—who desires to comprehend the meaning of holiness and live holy lives in today's world.

—Susie C. Stanley
Professor of Historical Theology, Messiah College, Grantham, Pennsylvania

Relational Holiness at last fills a gaping hole in books on holiness—a readable and accessible introduction that brings biblical, theological, and historical aspects together in language of the 21st century. This is for anyone who thinks holiness is important, isn't quite sure why it is important, or finds it all rather confusing but still wants to understand. And it will be invaluable for teachers of holiness who have not been able to find a straightforward treatment inside the covers of one book.

—Dwight D. Swanson
Senior Lecturer, Nazarene Theological College, Manchester, England

Wow—you guys have nailed it! You've taken the weary timbers of Holiness language and built an elegant edifice in which my friends and I can live gracefully, spacious enough for my incarcerated and seminary students alike.

The book disturbed what otherwise could have been a good night of sleep —one hour of reading and the rest of the night with the mind churned, the spirit fired, the passions stirred to jump into the dance with the Master dancer who invites us to join His life of holiness.

Congratulations! Timely! Well written! Tightly reasoned! Carefully and appropriately documented! Made practical with your pop questions and chapter bibliographies! And it comes out where it should—in "love" for God and fellow human beings.

—Fletcher Tink
Professor of Urban and Compassionate Ministries , Nazarene Theological Seminary
Executive Director, Bresee Institute for Metro Ministries, Kansas City

In a thriving and confident doctrinal tradition, voices will appear that can imaginatively, attractively, and faithfully rearticulate the genius that prompted its birth. In *Relational Holiness,* two talented churchmen and scholars have given fresh voice to the vision and life of Christian holiness. Used by the Spirit, their work will contribute to a winsome and compelling renewal of the doctrine of Christian holiness, a renewal upon which churches in the Holiness tradition always depend.

—Albert Truesdale
Professor Emeritus, Nazarene Theological Seminary, Kansas City

In *Relational Holiness,* Thomas J. Oord and Michael E. Lodahl set out the need for the Church to communicate clearly a Holiness theology of love to our 21st-century culture. The authors call us afresh to consider Wesley's "perfect love" as the critical integrative factor for the many facets of the doctrine of holiness. Today's world hungers for the sweet love of a relational holy God and His church. I commend this book to all pastors, teachers, and anyone who seeks to grow more deeply in understanding the holy ways of God.

—Charles E. Zink
Director of Clergy Development, Church of the Nazarene

RELATIONAL HOLINESS

Responding to the Call of Love

THOMAS JAY OORD AND MICHAEL LODAHL

Beacon Hill Press of Kansas City
Kansas City, Missouri

ISBN 083-412-1824

Printed in the
United States of America

Cover Design: Keith Alexander

Library of Congress Cataloging-in-Publication Data

Oord, Thomas Jay.
   Relational holiness : responding to the call of love / Thomas Jay Oord and Michael Lodahl.
      p. cm.
   Includes bibliographical references and index.
      ISBN 0-8341-2182-4 (pbk.)
   1. Holiness—Christianity. 2. Love—Religious aspects—Christianity. I. Lodahl, Michael E., 1955- II. Title.

   BT767.O73 2005
   234'.8—dc22

                                                            2005009775

10   9   8   7   6   5   4   3   2   1

Dedicated to
our family

the near and the distant,
the biological and the ecclesial,
the contemporary and the ancient.

As for our biological families, we have been very
fortunate to grow up within the loving nurture of our
Christian parents—sisters Virginia and Louise and their
respective husbands, Ken and Gene—and to share in the
heritage they have faithfully lived before and among us.

Of course, these good parents did not raise us and
our siblings without plenty of help. And much of that
help came from the saints of God at the Church
of the Nazarene in Othello, Washington.
In the words of the old hymn, "Blest be the
tie that binds our hearts in Christian love."

Contents

Foreword I

Holiness is—
full consecration of ourselves to God.
being sanctified holy.
being filled with the Spirit.
a second definite work of grace.
bearing the character of God in the world.
being set apart for the purposes of God.
being made perfect in love.
dying out to self.
being fully restored in the image of God.
purity of heart and life.
being part of a community of believers who by their
character bear witness in the world to the already-
not-yet kingdom of God.
loving God with our whole heart, soul, and mind, and
our neighbors as ourselves.
wholeness in Christ.
Christlikeness.

There are many different ways to talk about holiness in
the lives of believers. At least in part, this is because Scripture talks about holiness in many different ways. This may
at first seem to make holiness hard to understand and
even confusing. It may even seem as though people (even
preachers) are not talking about the same thing when

they use such different words and phrases to describe holiness.

Thomas Oord and Michael Lodahl help us sort this out. They point to the unifying principle or "core" that brings together all the different ways of talking about holiness. They help us understand that holiness in the lives of believers is grounded in the holy nature and character of God. In order to understand holiness in believers, we must understand holiness in the life of God.

Even here the discussion can become complex, because holiness in the life of God can be understood in several ways. It can include God's "wholly otherness" and spotless purity. Ultimately, however, these authors help us understand that God's holiness is all about God's love. The "core" of holiness is love. After all, God *is* love! When we talk about holiness as "relational love," other understandings of holiness fall into line.

Oord and Lodahl help us understand that this is not just God's love for us. It's God's nature of love in the life of the holy Trinity. That is, the love of God can first be understood as the love of the Father for the Son and Spirit, the love of the Son for the Father and Spirit, and the love of the Spirit for the Father and Son. The Persons of the Holy Trinity are related to one another in such a way that we can talk about them in terms of "mutually indwelling love." Because God's nature is love, it only makes sense that the Persons of the Holy Trinity would be interrelated in love.

This next point is especially exciting for those of us

who are believers. Our authors show that the God who is love and who is interrelated in love invites us to share in this life of divine love! Not only is God-in-Christ-Jesus-through-the-Spirit in us, but we are in God. We are invited to be partakers of the divine life! (See 2 Pet. 1:4.) And that life of holiness is, above all, a life of love. When we are part of God's life of love (and God's love is in us), there is room for nothing else—certainly no room for sin. We are filled with His Spirit, consecrated completely to God, sanctified "wholly." God's image of holiness is restored in us.

When we understand the core of holiness as love, the differing ways of talking about holiness begin to line up and make sense. Purity, being set apart for God's purposes, Christlikeness, love for God and for our neighbor—all these ways of talking about holiness in the lives of believers come together.

Many implications arise from this, not the least of which is the nature of our relationships in the Church. As God's holy character is "mutually indwelling love" and as we are invited to participate in God's holy life, we find we are not alone. There are others with us. Together as God's Church, we discover what it means to love one another as God loves us. In the same way that the Trinity is interrelated in love, the people of God, restored in God's image of holy love, are also interrelated in love.

In fact, one of the ways we know God's love is through the love of brothers and sisters in Christ. This love is more than something we talk about or think might happen somewhere, to some people, out there. God's love in the life of the Church is a love we personally experience and know to be true. We begin to understand what Jesus meant when He said that "everyone will know that you are my disciples, if you have love for one another" (John 13:35). And we have this love not only for one another but also for the world around us. As God loves the world, so do we.

All the while, it is God's love we are talking about. God's Spirit helps us along and shows us the way. This life of holiness is not something we know on our own. It is only by the Spirit that we can learn to walk with God in love and to live with one another as a people of love. For Oord and Lodahl, this is like a beautiful dance!

As you read the following pages, I invite you to pray that the Holy Spirit would lead you into God's truth about holiness. The following chapters are a guide, a map, a help in understanding holiness. But understanding holiness is only a first step. If you are to respond to God's invitation to a life of holiness, you must respond fully and obediently to the leading of the Spirit.

What a wonderful thing it is for us to be holy before God, participating in God's holy life and love, filled with God's love, and loving one another and all God's creation! The life of holiness is a life of holy love. Thanks be to God!

—Ron Benefiel
President, Nazarene Theological Seminary
Kansas City

Foreword II

It was the teaching of John Wesley that we are not free *for* perfect love until we are free *from* all sin, both outward and inward. While God's love is poured into our hearts by the Holy Spirit in the new birth, that love is "mixed" with remaining sinful self-love. Not until our hearts are purified from this lurking self-idolatry do we experience "pure love to God and man." Such has been the classic Wesleyan understanding of Christian holiness.

In Wesley's Standard Sermon "The Scripture Way of Salvation," however, which represents his mature understanding of entire sanctification, or Christian perfection, he seems to take a further step. Wesley explains the experience more holistically, defining it as the expulsive power of divine love. "Perfection," he says there, "is love excluding sin; love . . . taking up the whole capacity of the soul. . . . How clearly does this express the being perfected in love! How strongly imply the being saved from all sin! For as long as love takes up the whole heart, what room is there for sin therein?"

It is this positive, holistic view of Christian holiness that Thomas Oord and Michael Lodahl develop in this volume. By "relational holiness" they mean that we are born into a cosmos of relationships. To be human is to be inescapably related to God, creation, and others—and most important, to be encountered by God's prevenient grace.

Their approach tilts more toward John than Paul. While they cite Paul in several key passages, they delve more deeply into Jesus' teaching in John 14—17. In two brilliant, edifying chapters Tom and Mike spell out what it means to participate in the love of the triune God and to experience *koinonia* in the Church. These two chapters are more than worth the price of the book. I have long pondered Jesus' self-revelation in John 14—16 and His prayer for the Church in chapter 17, but these passages now minister to me in a new way. My prayer is that they will lead you deeply into the life of the Holy Trinity and of the Church as the mystical Body of Christ.

—William M. Greathouse
General Superintendent Emeritus, Church of the Nazarene

Preface I

The symphony of salvation is a marvelous experience punctuated by two powerful movements. The first movement encompasses the stirring chords of conviction, arresting the individual with a growing awareness of spiritual disequilibrium. For some, this spiritual dis-ease is accompanied by an awareness of God's invitation to leave one life and to enter something brand new. For others, it is an awareness of need, even guilt for a lifestyle contrary to the law of God.

This initial movement is accented with the subtle melodies of prevenient grace. Like an elegant accent underlying the dark chords of conviction, these subtle melodies track the progress of God's initiative in sending grace to heighten the impact of the towering chords of conviction. As the Holy Spirit works to awaken the individual to God's call, the Spirit creates intersections of grace. At each intersection, this *grace-that-goes-before* signals a strengthening reminder of God's invitation to new life in Christ. Curiously, to the individual, a force, unseen and perhaps even unknown, is arranging circumstances that if heeded and attended, will lead to new direction culminating in an inevitable life-changing decision.

The first movement in salvation's symphony reaches a powerful crescendo when personal decision and prevenient grace combine in a transformative moment. In this moment, we become God's new creation (2 Cor. 5:17). But this is not the end of the symphony—merely a punctuation point of powerful significance. This junction of themes (God's prevenient grace and our decisive acceptance of relationship marked by repentance and trust) hint at even more to come.

The second movement of the symphony of salvation builds upon the color, texture, and reality of all that has been ongoing from the beginning.

No symphonic masterpiece can be limited to one crescendo after another. Neither does God's masterpiece end with a grand crescendo marking the believer's justification, adoption, and new birth. God is working to express grace in the rhythmic contrasts of this new life experience. There are surface changes in the music God is creating in one's soul that hint at changes yet to come.

In this second movement, God begins the process of creating new experiences; new colors, sounds and rhythms begin to unfold. In this movement, the towering chords of conviction, dominated by the winds, are replaced by the articulating voices of the strings. In this relational journey is a profound sense of process leading to a juncture that culminates in a moment of surrender and consecration. This yieldedness signals the onset of a dynamic element in God's masterpiece wherein the Holy Spirit cleanses and purifies the believer's heart, filling it with a love that excludes all self-centeredness.

Despite the marked rhythmic differences of these two

movements, in reality they mirror a deeper, more profound truth. While the essence of God's grace cannot be subdivided into constituent parts, the movements by which God communicates grace to us can be marked by tracing the themes, phrases, and contrasts of this disarmingly simple melody. Holiness is the grand theme of God's relationship with creation! Reduced to its most simple expression, it is the story of love that embraces all of us and is expressed in the life, death, and resurrection of our Lord, Jesus Christ.

The basic structural elements of God's symphony combine within the context of these two movements to express grace and love. In turn, as participants along with God in this symphony, we give reality to the shadow of anticipation inherent in the message of the Good News. As our lives express love, we express the very essence of God's character: holiness.

The authors of this text assume the reader's knowledge of these two movements. Indeed, their work clarifies the profound significance of the Holiness message in ways that are clear and understandable. Perhaps the question confronting the reader is this: Have you responded to the movements of grace in your own life? Both movements are essential if one is to live in the relational holiness described in this work. Relational holiness is not the response of mere human decision. Indeed, it is the product of God's invasive grace, noted in the intersections of life and realized in the response of personal decision. Nor is relational holiness the predominant theme of a heart in which the clashing chords of self-sovereignty and Christ-likeness attempt an uneasy coexistence.

We commend the authors on their insightful analysis of holiness as love-in-relationship-with-God-and-others.

—David J. Felter
General Editor, Church of the Nazarene
Kansas City

Preface II

We offer *Relational Holiness* to help change present-day perceptions of holiness and sanctification. We want to return holiness to its rightful place of chief importance.

At least two passions drive us to write *Relational Holiness*. First, we are passionate about presenting holiness in a way that present and future generations will find believable, relevant, and truly good news. We believe that Holiness teaching best fulfills these goals when interpreted through the relational concept of *love*.

Second, we want to present holiness in a way that many Christians will understand. Being theological scholars, we know that specialized language often "flies right by" many people. We've set aside technical tangling to present this relational holiness framework in an understandable way.

In short, our first passion—communicating holiness in relational categories—fuels our second passion: to make holiness understandable today.

In one important sense, what we call relational holiness is a new paradigm for sanctification. If people find current understandings of holiness bewildering or irrelevant, perhaps the Holiness message couched in the relational categories of love can invigorate them.

In another sense, however, relational holiness is the

same "old" gospel found in the Bible, Christian tradition, contemporary experience, and especially the writings of John Wesley (1703-91). Our hope is that laypeople, pastors, and professors alike will find relational holiness theology both faithful to the ancient Christian message and applicable to how they understand God, others, and themselves.

Relational Holiness is written to be understood by a wide audience. But being the professors that we are, we also want to encourage some readers, especially our students, to dig deeper into the subjects we address. For this reason, we've added a bibliography of other writing on holiness at the end of each chapter.

We also hope that this book generates discussion outside university and college classrooms. To encourage this discussion, we've included questions at the conclusion of each chapter. We anticipate that small-group get-togethers, Bible studies, Sunday School classes, and those who gather in other ways will find that these questions spark creative dialogue about issues that matter most.

Acknowledgments

Many people have helped to make this book what it is. We wish to thank Jon Anderson, Robert Anderson, Susan Armstrong, Jena Atwood, Jeff Barker, Ron Benefiel, Dean Blevins, Phil Buck, Christi Butler, Carl Campbell, Zach Carpenter, Rhonda Carrim, Frank Carver, Steve Carroll, Kent Conrad, Tom Cornford, Scott Daniels, John DeBoer, Chris Desgroseillier, Darin Dodd, Ray Dunning, David Felter, Ahren Foster, Todd Fulcher, Bill Greathouse, the gym class at Nampa (Idaho) First Church of the Nazarene, Laura Hansen, Dana Hicks, Stan Ingersol, Chad Johnson, Jennie Johnston, Alisha Kafka, Tim Lanham, Christy Leppert, Rod Leupp, Joy Lindner, Janice Lodahl, Ernesto Lopez, Bob Luhn, Todd Lundberg, Brian Mackey, Mark Maddix, Randy Maddox, Jesse Maddux, Loren Maggard, Todd McArthur, Steve McCormick, Brant Meckel, Darren Melton, Jeff Miller, Troy Mishner, Ryan Morrison, Tom Nees, Ralph Neil, Cheryl Oord, Stephanie Pape, Michael Pate, Mary Rearick Paul, Karen Pearson, Mark Pitts, Darrell Poeppelmeyer, Jerry Porter, Mark Porterfield, Jonathan Ralph, Todd Renegar, Ryan Roberts, Ed Robinson, Trevor Robinson, Carol Rotz, Jeren Rowell, Bethany Sanders, Carla Schreffler, Josh Shultz, Mary Lou Shea, Samantha Shea, Susie Stanley, Rob Staples, LeAnn Stensgaard, James Sullivan, Angela Swanson, Barry Swanson,

Dwight Swanson, Chris Tiner, Fletcher Tink, Dave Tolson, Kevin Tompos, Michael Tonn, Tiffany Triplett, Al Truesdale, Michael Turner, Jason Vickers, Reg Watson, Kyle Yake, Gail Zickefoose, and Chuck Zink.

We especially thank Nancy Pitts and Tom Phillips.

The list above indicates a small portion of the Christian family to which we owe a great deal. We are also indebted to a long history of Christian thinkers who have contributed to our understanding of what it means to be a Christian. This book would not be written were it not for the Church.

1
Pygmies
and Atoms

The classical terms of holiness—"Christian perfection," "entire sanctification," "the second blessing," and "baptism of the Holy Spirit"—no longer seize the imaginations of many people. Evidence of this is found chiefly in the fact that Christian leaders both inside and outside the Holiness tradition rarely use these terms today. Laypeople use them even less.

Perhaps we in the Holiness tradition are becoming like the Myanmar pygmies.

At the beginning of the 21st century, conservationist Alan Rabinowitz set out to explore the remote mountain regions of Myanmar. Prior to 1989, this relatively unexplored nation was known as Burma. Rabinowitz wanted to document species of indigenous animals largely unknown to the outside world. Myanmar officials supported the venture, because they knew little about the plants, animals, and even some people living in the isolated mountains areas.

Prior to setting out on the excursion, Rabinowitz happened across long-forgotten reports on the region written in the late 1950s and early 1960s. These reports mentioned a tribe of approximately 100 pygmies living in the Myanmar mountains. This tribe apparently contained the world's only pygmies of Asian ancestry. Rabinowitz realized that since the writing of these reports nearly four decades earlier, no one from outside the region had documented the state of this hidden and peculiar tribe.

After searching the deep mountain valleys for some time, Rabinowitz found the pygmy people. He regretted to discover, however, that only about a dozen of these dwarfish humans still existed. The genetic lineage of only three remained pure, and these three had decided not to marry. This peculiar race was within a few years of extinction.

Rabinowitz spoke with the youngest remaining pygmy, a 39-year-old bachelor named Dawi. He asked Dawi why the pygmies were nearing total disappearance. In his response, the pygmy male noted the high infant mortality rate and increased probability of mental illness that typically accompany inbreeding. But he also told Rabinowitz that his people had consciously chosen not to reproduce to continue their lineage. Or, as Rabinowitz put it, these people "had become active participants in their own extinction."

The pygmies of Myanmar could have chosen to reinvigorate their disappearing race. Their genetic relatives lived not far away in China. Although the Chinese relatives were not pygmies, their genetic lineage could have continued through intermarriage with these next of kin.

The pygmies also could have intermarried with non-pygmies of their native mountain region. These matrimonies could have been orchestrated so that the pygmies would not have lost their cultural and social identity, despite relinquishing their genetic purity.

The Myanmar pygmies, however, chose neither to retain their identity as a people nor to adapt to their changing environment. A vision for a prosperous future failed to seize their imaginations. And without such a vision, this unique people literally perished.

Perhaps the fundamental identity of the Holiness Movement—its theological distinctive—is also becoming extinct. Perhaps it is only the organizational machinery that keeps the tradition alive, while its theology no longer exerts influence.

Like the pygmies, Christians attending Holiness churches have felt the negative influence of forces beyond their control. But the way that Christians understand holiness—or perhaps their general *lack* of understanding—has likely been the most important factor in their failure of imagination. That factor *is* within their control. Could it be that Holiness people are passive participants—and at times even active participants—in the looming extinction of their own theological heritage?

Today both those inside and outside the Holiness Movement get the impression that holiness has become an irrelevant or extra dimension to contemporary Christian life. As one young man put it, "Why worry about being holy or about entire santifi . . . uh, what did you call that? . . . when what the world really needs is Jesus? Besides, I don't recall Jesus using those terms."

Many of the most passionate Holiness advocates from yesteryear would not be surprised that many today regard holiness as passé. Early Holiness leaders worried about what future generations would do with what these leaders considered the distinctive doctrine of their faith.

Today students raised in the Holiness tradition arrive at colleges and universities having heard little if anything about holiness and sanctification. And those who have heard the terms typically identify them with some negative aspect of religion they want to avoid. Holiness seems no longer to be a central concern for younger generations.

At least in North America, denominations with ties to the Holiness tradition are in danger of becoming theologically unrecognizable from the Evangelical Christian mainstream. To be sure, some in Holiness circles have treated what are actually theological molehills like mountains. And this practice has unnecessarily divided Holiness advocates from the broader Evangelical community.

Even so, it now seems as important as ever to clarify what if anything distinguishes Holiness Christians from others. Unless distinctions that identify real differences are named, the denominations that comprise the Holiness tradition may as well fade into mainstream Evangelicalism. They may as well allow the Holiness story to become a curious historical footnote—like that of the Myanmar pygmies.

A general superintendent in the Church of the Nazarene summed up well the state of affairs in North America's largest Holiness denomination. Apparently speaking for other leaders in the movement, the superintendent said at an early-21st-century global theology conference, "We believe that our denomination is currently in a theological crisis." An important book about the Holiness Movement published at about that same time concluded that "the question in the last decades of the 20th century was whether or not the Church of the Nazarene had a coherent and cogent doctrine of holiness at all."*

Several analysts offer explanations for the diminishing interest in holiness. Some say that heirs of the Holiness tradition have become preoccupied with fitting into the Christian mainstream, a stream that itself reserves little place for Holiness language. Others suggest that being holy requires being out of step with society, and Holiness people have become more interested in appearing reputable. Some say that church growth models undermine the theological focus on holiness. Some argue that holiness—understood as perfection, sanctification, and so on—is not now and has never been an adequate basis on which to establish an entire Christian theological trajectory. Additional reasons have been proposed.

These and other explanations may have a degree of validity. The thesis of this book, however, is that the *main* reason many lack interest in the doctrine of holiness has

*Mark A. Quanstrom, *A Century of Holiness Theology: The Doctrine of Entire Sanctification in the Church of the Nazarene: 1905 to 2004* (Kansas City: Beacon Hill Press of Kansas City, 2004), 169.

to do with the interplay between theological assumptions and contemporary worldviews.

The truth is that people today view their world in radically different ways than did people 100, 50, or even 20 years ago. A worldview change has occurred. It has become vogue to label this shift "postmodernism." Although understandings of postmodernism vary, the belief that people view the world differently than their predecessors unites these varying understandings.

This shift in worldview means that even if the forebearers of holiness spoke with one voice about what it meant to be sanctified, we would still need a fresh proposal for how holiness might best be understood today. It is futile simply to recycle Holiness sermons and literature from yesteryear in hopes that the old-style Holiness Movement might revive.

In this book, we intend to return holiness to its place of chief importance while presenting its core meaning in an understandable and biblically faithful way. Because societies around the world change, the core Christian message—holiness—must be presented in new ways and with new language so as to seize our hearts and imaginations. The Christian gospel must be contextualized for the present age without compromising its core.

We believe that we must reassert the theological importance of holiness. To do this, we offer a Holiness vision to seize hearts and imaginations for what can be a prosperous future. But before we address holiness specifically and argue for its chief importance, we need to look briefly at contemporary worldviews.

A RELATIONAL WORLDVIEW

If we could choose one word to summarize how many people view their world today—the postmodern world— that word would be "relational." Even visions of postmodernism that largely oppose each other share this emphasis upon relationality.

Before further explaining what a relational worldview entails, we should lay to rest a few common misconceptions about relational ways of thinking. When we talk about possessing a relational worldview, we are not talking about being sociable or friendly. To see the world in relational terms does not necessarily have to do with caring, congeniality, or getting along with others—although the world would surely be a better place if we expressed such pro-social behavior.

We see elements of the relational worldview in diverse domains. It prevails in the sciences, for instance, from physics to biology to psychology to political science and various disciplines in between. In these and other domains, it is becoming common to talk about our world as composed of entities or subjects that exist in mutual relations, whether we're thinking of a tree, a whale, a person, a star, a proton, or anything else. Many understand meaning itself as having to do with identifying the relations between one thing and another.

A relational worldview considers things and persons as deeply interconnected. To "be" is to be in relation. An individual's relations with others largely decide what that individual is. To say it another way, it belongs to the nature of everything that exists—indeed, of *existence itself*—to be related and for those relations to affect the fundamental nature of existing things.

Even with this short description of a relational worldview, one can guess that it greatly affects how we understand what it means to be a person. Many contemporary people understand personhood to be the history of the interactions and the choices that individuals make. This is a relational understanding of personhood.

The relations that an individual has with his or her environment—social, familial, political, physical, natural, religious, mental, and so on—largely shape that individual's being and character. Some describe humans today with phrases such as "persons-in-community," "individuals-in-relation," or even "community-created-persons." These descriptions are an attempt to capture the fundamental importance of our relatedness to others.

Of course, individuals are not wholly determined by the relations they have with others or their environments. We all exercise at least some degree of agency with limited freedom in response to others. But powerful environmental factors determine the range of choices we entertain at any given time. How we respond to these factors and relations influences who we become.

We believe that Christians should find relational postmodernism particularly helpful for talking about our relation to God. Christians can agree wholeheartedly with the postmodern view that persons become who they are out of decisions made in response to their relational environ-ments. Believers argue, however, that our environment in-cludes a Presence not acknowledged by unbelievers.

It certainly fits with this postmodern emphasis upon relations for Christians to contend that God acts as an ever-present, divine influence—a necessary cause—in everyone's relational environment. Just as people affect others through relations, God as the Maker and Sustainer of all things also affects all things, all people, all the time, everywhere. There is no environment in which God is not related to others as a present, active, and loving agent.

To think about God in this way is to believe that God is the most important actor in everyone's environment. God affects *all* others and does so in every moment. This is a significant part of what Wesley and others have called "prevenient grace." This grace, which is none other than God, surrounds and sustains every one of us, all the time (cf. Acts 17:28). And by this relational grace all things exist.

Many postmodernists reject the claim that we can know our world solely from what we learn from taste, touch, sight, smell, and hearing. They talk about the im-portance of intuition—also known as tacit or personal knowledge—to supplement and enrich the knowledge gained from our five senses. Some postmodernists even speak of nonsensory perception to account for this knowledge, and this perceptive activity is perhaps exem-plified best by the perceiving we do with our minds. When we remember the past, we perceive something real with-out using our five senses.

This postmodern way of talking about how we come to know our world fits nicely with Christian traditions that speak of the Holy Spirit communicating with our spirits. The intuitive communication of postmodernism seems identical at least in technique with the biblical accounts of human interaction with the God who cannot be seen, touched, tasted, smelled, or audibly heard. For God is spirit (John 4:24).

The postmodern idea of a moment-by-moment relational existence provides the key to a contemporary Christian conception of life. According to this idea, each moment of life begins by being influenced by the past. History—both what occurred the previous moment and what occurred in the distant past—influences the present.

Each person in each moment chooses among a variety of options and alternatives based upon his or her relations with the past. The choice one makes in any particular moment is a response to what is immediately possible given that person's environment. That choice contributes to the becoming of that person and also contributes to that person's relations in the future.

In this way of looking at things, persons are relational through and through. They are related to others and to what has come before as the past impinges upon them. They are related to others in the present. Those who will come after them will relate to them as influences upon their own future personhood.

In the midst of it all, God is also present and acting relationally. No one, including God, is wholly independent or isolated from others. God is not entirely independent, because God is love, and love is expressed in relationships. Relationships require a kind of dependence if they are true relationships.

To exist, of course, God does not depend upon creatures. God was not born and will not die; God does not depend upon others in order to be. Rather, to say that God is dependent is to affirm the relational dependence that love requires. To rejoice with those who rejoice and mourn with those who mourn requires an experiential dependence. A God of love desires and seeks this kind of dependent relation.

God is open to and affected by others, because the Creator and the creatures enjoy mutual relations. To say that these relations are mutual is to say that God interacts with us and we interact with God. Mutuality is not the same as equality, however. God is not another mortal; there are numerous differences between the Creator and the creatures. But the wonder of it all is that the God of the universe enjoys give-and-take relations with every creature who lives.

Our descriptions of God will not and cannot be exhaustive. While Christians believe that some important things can be said about their Maker and Savior, they typically don't claim to have given a full explanation of what divinity entails. Nevertheless, more and more people believe that the description of God as relational resides at the heart of how best to describe the Lover of us all. And they believe that this description can be enormously helpful in teaching us what it might mean to love one another.

Perhaps we can begin to see that this relational world-view will affect how we understand some of the most basic issues of our existence. And if holiness belongs among the most basic issues, it seems likely that a relational view of holiness—*relational* holiness—might affect the way we think, talk, and act as Christians in a postmodern world.

But we are starting to get ahead of ourselves. A more detailed explanation of relational holiness waits in the chapters that follow.

CORE AND CONTRIBUTING NOTIONS

There is another factor that contributes to the inability of holiness to seize contemporary imaginations. It is that diverse concepts of holiness exist.

It is not uncommon for a person to grow up in the Holiness tradition, attend a Holiness college or university, and proceed even to a Holiness seminary, all the while finding that theologians in the Holiness tradition have come to differing conclusions about what holiness means. We will see in the following chapter that one reason for this plurality is the diversity of the Bible itself. At present, we need acknowledge only that leaders within the Holiness tradition offer significantly different understandings of holiness.

The Holiness Movement needs an interpretative framework that will order the chaos of meanings and make the heart of holiness understandable. This interpretative framework should be grounded primarily in Scripture. But it will also incorporate reason, Christian tradition, and contemporary experiences.

In this book we will suggest a way of understanding holiness that integrates diverse notions of holiness. We call the concept that integrates the other meanings of holiness "the core notion of holiness." While the other meanings of holiness are important, they represent contributing notions rather than the core.

Perhaps an analogy will help us understand the relation between the core notion and the contributing notions that it encompasses. Nearly 3,000 years ago, the earliest Western philosophers wondered what the most fundamental unit of existence might be. Thales, perhaps the earliest philosopher, thought that water was the most fundamental. It appeared to him that all of life depends upon water, and water can be found in almost everything. Therefore, he surmised, the most basic element of existence must be water.

Anaximenes started a speculative debate with the followers of Thales a few generations later. Anaximenes suggested that air was more basic than water. After all, water seems to be partially comprised of air, and air can be found in almost everything. Anaximenes thus concluded that air must be the most fundamental element of existence.

Heraclitus followed these two philosophers. Although he was mainly interested in noting that all things change, Heraclitus also joined the discussion by considering what the most basic unit of existence might be. For him, fire was more basic than either air or water, because fire reveals that existence has both stability and change.

Other early philosophers entered the debate. Many suggested that the most fundamental element of existence is dirt, or dust. From dust we came, and from dust we shall return. So dirt must be most basic.

These four elements—water, air, fire, and dirt—vied for the role of ultimate explanation for everything. Each pointed to some important truth evident to common experience. But none of the four encompassed the truths of the others. When any one element was suggested to be the most basic, it became apparent that it was woefully inadequate at encompassing the truths expressed by the other three.

Into the history of philosophy came someone whose idea integrated the others. That someone was Democritus, and he argued that existence is fundamentally composed of atoms. Water, air, fire, and earth all are made up of these atoms.

Democritus's proposal won the day, because it proved to be an adequate explanatory principle. His atomic theory incorporated the truths expressed by those who had come before. Because of Democritus, scientists today still speak of the atom—although they often also use other terms to avoid the connotations that the concept of the atom carries over from previous centuries.

This true story of how atomic theory emerged in competition with other theories illustrates what we want to say about the relationship between the core and contributing notions of holiness. Contributing notions express something true, but they are inadequate in themselves for capturing the other truths that must be represented.

When contributing notions are treated as core notions, problems arise. Contributing notions cannot carry the full weight required of the core notion. And it becomes difficult for us to defend wholeheartedly the truth of a contributing notion when it pretends to fill the role that only the core notion can fill.

The core notion incorporates the truths that various contributing notions express without negating those varying truths. And the core notion becomes the bottom-line explanation to which one ultimately appeals. When an adequate core notion is found, contributing notions become more valuable as they fulfill their proper place of support. In many cases, contributing notions specify in their own ways the more general truth expressed in the core notion.

With some of the differences between core and contributing notions in mind, we are ready to move ahead. We turn to examine the meanings of holiness.

QUESTIONS TO STIMULATE DISCUSSION

1. What do you understand to be the significance of the terms "Christian perfection," "entire sanctification," "the second blessing," and "the baptism of the Holy Spirit"?

2. Do you find that Holiness groups are *theologically* unrecognizable from the Evangelical Christian mainstream? Is this a good or bad thing?

3. Why do you think some today have little interest in holiness? On what would you blame this lack of interest?

4. How did you learn about holiness and what it meant?

5. What were some of the basic beliefs of the relational worldview presented in this chapter? Of what importance might they be for holiness?

6. Can you summarize what the authors mean by core and contributing notions?

7. Guess: What do you think the authors will claim is the core notion of holiness? Why do you think the core notion will be what you have guessed?

FOR DEEPER STUDY

Boone, Dan. "Our Story Tells Us Who We Are." In *Holiness 101: Exploring This Transforming Journey*. Kansas City: Beacon Hill Press of Kansas City, 2003.

Creasman, Ronald. "The Loss of Metanarrative: Resources for Formulating a Wesleyan Response." *Wesleyan Theological Journal* 35:1 (spring 2000).

Crutcher, Timothy. "Labels, Assumptions, and a Generation Called 'X.'" In *Generation Xers Talk About the Church of the Nazarene*. Edited by Thomas Jay Oord. Kansas City: Beacon Hill Press of Kansas City, 1999.

Drury, Keith. *The Holiness Movement: Dead or Alive?* (An edited combination of his essays "The Holiness Movement Is Dead" and "Hope for the Holiness Movement"), <www.cresourcei.org/hmovement.html>.

Dunning, H. Ray. "Holiness: Experience or Relationship?" In *Holiness 101: Exploring This Transforming Journey*. Kansas City: Beacon Hill Press of Kansas City, 2003.

Hicks, Dana. "On Being Neo-Nazarene." In *Generation Xers Talk About the Church of the Nazarene*. Edited by Thomas Jay Oord. Kansas City: Beacon Hill Press of Kansas City, 1999.

Kelle, Brad E. "A Postmodern Church for a Postmodern Generation." In *Generation Xers Talk about the Church of the Nazarene*. Edited by Thomas Jay Oord. Kansas City: Beacon Hill Press of Kansas City, 1999.

Kostlvey, William C., ed. *Historical Dictionary of the Holiness Movement*. Lanham, Md.: Scarecrow Press, 2001.

Maddox, Randy L. "Reconnecting the Means to the End: A Wesleyan Prescription for the Holiness Movement." *Wesleyan Theological Journal*, 33.2 (1998).

Mann, Mark Grear. "Religious Pluralism." In *Philosophy of Religion: Introductory Essays*. Kansas City: Beacon Hill Press of Kansas City, 2003.

McKenna, David. *What a Time to Be Wesleyan! Proclaiming the Holiness Message with Passion and Purpose*. Kansas City: Beacon Hill Press of Kansas City, 1999.

Meeks, Douglas M. "Wesleyan Theology in a Postmodern Era: The Spirit of Life in an Age of the Nihil." *Wesleyan Theological Journal* 35:1 (spring 2000).

Miller, William Charles. *Holiness Works: A Bibliography*. Kansas City: Nazarene Theological Seminary, 1986.

Moore, Frank. *Breaking Free from Sin's Grip: Holiness Defined for a New Generation*. Kansas City: Beacon Hill Press of Kansas City, 2001.

Oord, Thomas Jay, ed. *Generation Xers Talk About the Church of the Nazarene*. Kansas City: Beacon Hill Press of Kansas City, 1999.

———. "Postmodernism: What Is It?" In *Didache: Faithful Teaching: Exploring the Intersections of Christian Conviction, Culture and Education* 1:2 (winter 2000), <www.nazarene.org/iboe/riie/Didache/didache_vol1_2/postmodernism1.html>.

———. "Prevenient Grace and Nonsensory Perception of God in a Postmodern Wesleyan Philosophy." In *Between Nature and Grace: Mapping the Interface of Wesleyan Theology and Psychology*. San Diego: Point Loma Nazarene University, 2000.

Pinnock, Clark H. "Evangelical Theologians Facing the Future: Ancient and Future Paradigms." *Wesleyan Theological Journal* 33:2 (fall 1998).

Powell, Samuel M. *Holiness in the 21st Century: Call, Consecration, Obedience Perfected in Love*. San Diego: Point Loma Nazarene University, 2004.

Price, James Matthew. "H. Orton Wiley—Dominant Images From the Life of a Holiness Educator." *Wesleyan Theological Journal* 39:2 (fall 2004).

Quanstrom, Mark. *A Century of Holiness Theology: The Doctrine of Entire Sanctification in the Church of the Nazarene: 1905 to 2004*. Kansas City: Beacon Hill Press of Kansas City, 2004.

"Reminting Christian Holiness." Web site at <holiness.nazarene.ac.uk>.

Robinson, Ed. "A Generation of Opportunity." In *Generation Xers Talk about the Church of the Nazarene*. Edited by Thomas Jay Oord. Kansas City: Beacon Hill Press of Kansas City, 1999.

Short, Chad. "Wesleyan Theology and the Postmodern Quest for Meaning and Identity." *Wesleyan Theological Journal*. 39:2 (fall 2004).

Spaulding, Henry W. II. "Faith and Reason." In *Philosophy of Religion: Introductory Essays*. Edited by Thomas Jay Oord. Kansas City: Beacon Hill Press of Kansas City, 2003.

Stanley, Susie C., "Bumping into Modernity: Primitive/Modern Tensions in the Wesleyan/Holiness Movement." In *The Primitive Church in the Modern World*. Edited by Richard T. Hughes. Urbana, Ill.: University of Illinois Press, 1995.

——— with Jean Stockard and Benton Johnson. "Moving from Sect to Church: Variations in Views Regarding Sanctification Among Wesleyan/Holiness Clergy." *Review of Religious Research* 43:1 (September 2001).

Staples, Rob L. "Holiness—Core Questions, Straight Answers." In *Holiness 101: Exploring This Transforming Journey*. Kansas City: Beacon Hill Press of Kansas City, 2003.

———. "Sanctification and Selfhood: A Phenomenological Analysis of the Wesleyan Message." *Wesleyan Theological Journal* 7:1 (spring 1972).

Stone, Bryan P. "Process and Sanctification." In *Thy Nature and Thy Name Is Love: Wesleyan and Process Theologies in Dialogue*. Edited by Bryan P. Stone and Thomas Jay Oord. Nashville: Kingswood Books, 2001.

Taylor, Richard S. "Why the Holiness Movement Died." *God's Revivalist*, 1999.

Thomas, Gordon J. "Who Cares About Holiness Anyhow?" In *Holiness 101: Exploring This Transforming Journey*. Kansas City: Beacon Hill Press of Kansas City, 2003.

Thorsen, Don. "Reuniting the Two So Long Disjoined: Knowledge and Vital Piety." In *Heart of the Heritage*. Edited by Barry L. Callen and William C. Kostlevy. Salem, Ohio: Schmul Publishing Co., 2001.

Tink, Fletcher L. "Sanctification and the 'Burbs." *Holiness Today*, April 2002.

Truesdale, Albert. "Reification of the Experience of Entire Sanctification in the American Holiness Movement." *Wesleyan Theological Journal*, fall 1996.

Wetmore, A. Gordon. "Holiness: That the World May Know God." *The Tower: The Journal of Nazarene Theological Seminary* 4 (2000).

Wynkoop, Mildred Bangs. "The Credibility Gap." In *A Theology of Love: The Dynamic of Wesleyanism*. Kansas City: Beacon Hill Press of Kansas City, 1972.

2
Searching for the Core

Both the pope and the Dalai Lama are often given the label "His Holiness." Muslims insist on calling the Qu'ran a holy book. Some suggest a particular Christian movement be called "the Holiness tradition." Many citizens of planet Earth confess that holiness is their deepest heart cry.

But what is holiness? And what does it mean to be holy?

DIVERSITY IN SCRIPTURE

Christians believe that the meaning of holiness and sanctification must be found in the Bible if they are to consider these terms central to faith. After all, Christians look to Scripture as their principal authority when it comes to theology. The Bible must provide the foundation and framework upon which they construct a viable understanding of holiness. This doctrine must be the heart of the biblical message if Christians are to regard holiness and sanctification as anything more than extraneous sentiment or pious fluff.

The most obvious way to search for the biblical meaning of holiness is the word-study approach. This method identifies passages in the Bible that contain the words "holy," "holiness," "sanctification," and the like.

A study of references pertaining to holiness, sanctification, and related words, however, provides surprising results. The surprise, at least for those who have not done this search, is that the Bible offers a wide array of ideas about holiness and sanctification.

Below is a small sample of what one can find when using the word-study approach to identify the meaning of "holiness" and "sanctification." As you read through each passage, consider what the author might mean. Certain words are printed in bold for emphasis.

The author of Hebrews writes, "Jesus also suffered outside the city gate in order to **sanctify** the people by his own blood" (13:12).

Jesus asks his critics, "Can you say that the one whom the Father has **sanctified** and sent into the world is blaspheming because I said, 'I am God's Son'?" (John 10:36).

Paul designates a letter "to the church of God that is in Corinth, to those who are **sanctified** in Christ Jesus," and yet he calls these same people "infants in Christ" who are not ready for solid food (1 Cor. 1:2; 3:1).

Peter authors a letter to exiled Christians "who have been chosen and destined by God the Father and **sanctified** by the Spirit to be obedient to Jesus Christ." Although sanctified, he instructs them to "be **holy** yourselves in all your conduct; for it is written, 'You shall be **holy,** for I am **holy**'"

(1 Pet. 1:2, 15-16). Later in the same letter, Peter instructs his readers, "In your hearts **sanctify** Christ as Lord" (3:15).

Paul instructs Corinthian believers, "Let us cleanse ourselves from every defilement of body and of spirit, making **holiness** perfect in the fear of God" (2 Cor. 7:1).

The writers of Exodus record God instructing the priests to "make atonement for the altar, and consecrate it, and the altar shall be most **holy**; whatever touches the altar shall become **holy**" (29:37).

Paul tells believers in Rome "to be a minister in Christ Jesus to the Gentiles in the priestly service of the gospel of God, so that the offering of the Gentiles may be acceptable, **sanctified** by the Holy Spirit" (Rom. 15:16).

To the church in Thessalonica, Paul writes, "May the Lord make you increase and abound in love for one another and for all, just as we abound in love for you. And may he so strengthen your hearts in **holiness** that you may be blameless" (1 Thess. 3:12-13).

The Levites record God as saying, "I am the LORD your God; **sanctify** yourselves therefore, and be **holy**, for I am **holy**" (Lev. 11:44).

Paul says that "the unbelieving husband is made **holy** through his wife, and the unbelieving wife is made **holy** through her husband." In addition, children are made **holy** through their parents (1 Cor. 7:14).

Timothy is told that even food is "**sanctified** by God's word and by prayer" (1 Tim. 4:5).

John reports Jesus asking God to **sanctify** the disciples (17:17). Subsequent to that request, Jesus says that "for their sakes I **sanctify** myself, so that they also may be **sanctified** in truth" (17: 19).

Paul writes to the Ephesians: "Husbands, love your wives, just as Christ loved the church and gave himself up for her, in order to make her **holy** by cleansing her with the washing of water by the word, so as to present the church to himself in splendor, without spot or wrinkle or anything of the kind—yes, so that she may be **holy** and without blemish" (Eph. 5:25-27).

A number of interesting matters emerge in this sampling. We find biblical passages stating that Christ makes people holy, believers can make themselves holy, believers can make unbelievers holy, and altars can make offerings (not necessarily people) holy. We find that the Holy Spirit can sanctify, people should sanctify themselves, God sanctifies Jesus, Jesus sanctifies himself, and Jesus asks God to sanctify disciples. We discover that Jesus needed to be sanctified, food can be sanctified, people can be sanctified, unbelievers can be sanctified, and the Church is sanctified.

These passages and others throughout the Bible reveal a variety of meanings for holiness and sanctification. In particular, a survey of the biblical literature reveals that sometimes authors use the words "holy," "holiness," and/or "sanctification" to talk about

- following rules and ethical codes;
- being pure, clean, or without blemish;
- being set apart;
- total devotion or complete commitment;

- perfection;
- love.

The word-study approach shows that more than one meaning of "holiness" presents itself for consideration. In fact, the Bible contains a plurality of meanings for "holiness" and "sanctification."

Of course, a thorough analysis of these meanings would require in-depth contextual examinations of each passage in which the meanings are found. The words "holy," "holiness," and "sanctification" appear about a thousand times in the Bible. Therefore, an analysis of them all is beyond the scope of this book. But after one analyzes every one of them (and a few scholars have done this), the fact remains that a decided lack of uniformity exists.

This diversity of meanings should make us realize that understanding these terms requires more than just looking up verses in the Bible. The word-study approach doesn't go nearly far enough. Instead, we must make various interpretive decisions in order to identify the main themes of Scripture. In short, we must don our systematic theology hats while working with the biblical text if we are to provide an adequate framework for understanding holiness and sanctification.

The systematic theologian does not allow the multiple meanings of "holiness" to remain disconnected and incoherent. Allowing the plurality to remain muddled only fosters a state of confusion, disunity, and error. Such a state is one reason the Holiness Movement is currently in a crisis over its theological identity.

The sympathetic reader of Scripture may respond to its plurality by claiming that this only reveals the rich diversity of meanings of holiness found in the Bible. This response seems justified, however, only if one also suggests a common theme that underlies or ties together this diversity. Otherwise, it becomes difficult to distinguish what the sympathetic reader calls the Bible's rich diversity from what the unsympathetic reader calls confusion and chaos.

The systematic theologian seeks to identify an inclusive understanding of holiness. Although seeking order and consistency is his or her job, the systematic theologian leans heavily upon biblical scholars, historians, philosophers, and scientists of various types for this integrative work.

Identifying an inclusive understanding of holiness is the key to seeing how the diverse meanings of the Bible share some common theme. This sought-after inclusive understanding of holiness—what we earlier called "the core notion of holiness"—offers the interpretive key for recognizing an overarching unity that connects the plurality. It would be the atom that underlies water, air, fire, and dirt.

Several understandings of holiness offer themselves as candidates to carry the banner "the core notion of holiness." In the remainder of this chapter, we address the most promising candidates and ask if they can serve well as the core.

HOLINESS AS RULES AND REGULATIONS

It is perfectly natural for children to understand the Christian faith as having primarily to do with following rules. Psychologists tell us that children lack the brain development necessary for abstract thinking and global reasoning. Knowing and following rules requires little or nothing in the way of abstract thinking and global reasoning.

Additionally, biblical reasons exist for understanding holiness as following rules and regulations. For instance, biblical scholars have often labeled the rules listed in Leviticus, especially in chapters 17-26, as "the Holiness Code." Various actions are called holy. Things and objects are deemed holy. And God is said to be holy. The lists of commands are long, however, and following them would appear tedious and often irrelevant to Christians of even the earliest generations, not to mention those of the present era.

Several problems arise when we regard the core meaning of holiness and sanctification as following rules and regulations. Many reared in the Holiness tradition are keenly aware of these problems. Perhaps chief among them is the tendency toward legalism. Legalism is lethal to holiness.

The Pharisees were apparently holy in the sense that they kept all the rules commanded of them. But Jesus had harsh words for legalists who knew well how to cross their ethical "t's" and dot their moral "i's" but did not love. "Woe to you, scribes and Pharisees, hypocrites!" said Jesus. "For you tithe mint, dill, and cummin, and have neglected the weightier matters of the law: justice and mercy and faith" (Matt. 23:23). Jesus seems to be indicating that laws are means to an end. Rules and regulations are not ends in themselves.

Other problems arise when we regard the keeping of rules and regulations as core notion of holiness. For instance, those who keep the rules report feeling a lack of deep satisfaction for their efforts. The keeping of rules in itself does not bring meaning to life. Many report that they have been paralyzed by the fear that they will go to hell if they failed to keep every command. This approach to holiness also often fosters a judgmental and critical spirit toward those who do not follow all the rules strictly.

While ethical codes play an important role for understanding holiness, we conclude that they cannot function as the core notion. Rules and regulations must serve as contributing elements to an adequate understanding of holiness.

The Purity Concern

Related to understanding holiness as keeping rules—yet distinct from it—is the idea that holiness has to do with purity and cleanliness. Paul urges his Christian companions in Corinth to "cleanse [them]selves from every defilement of body and of spirit, making holiness perfect in the fear of God" (2 Cor. 7:1).

The idea of being pure appeals to most people. We feel revitalized and refreshed after rinsing off the sweat and grime we accumulate while toiling at some task—and others around us are grateful as well! The act of becoming clean (and the feeling of rejuvenation that often accompanies it) serves as a powerful metaphor for being rid of sin.

The desire to be pure is especially strong when we consider the consequences of our sexual sins. Many of us have engaged in sexual activity that we now find shameful. And the thought patterns we may have developed because of pornography leave us feeling dirty and polluted. We long for the chance to be given a clean slate. We desperately want the obscene movies that play in our heads erased. We want these sexual viruses erased from our hard drives. If being holy means having the lingering garbage of sexual sin eliminated, we want holiness.

There are a number of problems that arise, however, when we consider purity the core notion of holiness. One of these problems is conceptual, and it is linked to the worldview issues we addressed in the previous chapter. The conceptual problem is that purity is chiefly a static, rather than relational, category. The best examples of purity are nonpersonal, relatively static objects. *sterile*

For instance, it is easy to talk about honey as pure. We can imagine a glass of pure water. Biblical authors typically speak of purity when referring to nonpersonal objects such as cups, sheets, linens, altars, and other articles.

It is much more difficult to talk about living organisms as pure. After all, when was the last time you heard someone say that a mouse or cat was pure? And can you imagine what a pure chimpanzee would be? We may talk about an animal's genetic lineage being pure, but we typically consider genes impersonal. Persons are relational and constantly changing, so it seems strange to use the static category of purity.

As soon as we talk about humans as pure, we almost

inevitably slip back to using moral categories—a topic we covered in the previous section. And talking about purity by using moral categories typically leads to talking about holiness in terms of keeping rules and regulations.

A further problem emerges when we assume purity to be the core notion of holiness. The emphasis upon purity and remaining pure inclines us to focus solely upon avoiding sin rather than also upon doing good. Instead of engaging our world—including befriending the vilest of sinners—those who concentrate on remaining pure tend to *withdraw* from the world. Like turtles, they retreat into their own sanitary shells. Although they are not *of* the world, neither are they *in* it.

The idea that "I don't smoke, drink, chew, or go with guys [or girls] who do" is a reactive rather than proactive approach to life. Just as an emphasis upon holiness as following rules tends toward legalism, an emphasis upon holiness as purity tends toward disengagement and isolationism.

In the end we ask, "What is the redemptive value of purity? What is the purpose of being pure?" Perhaps in answering questions such as these we will discover the core notion of holiness. In the meantime, we conclude that while purity plays an important role in holiness, it cannot function as its core notion. Purity remains a contributing element in the grand framework of sanctification.

SET APART AND SEPARATION

Most people don't know that the biblical writers use the Hebrew word *qodesh* and the Greek word *hagios* to talk about holiness, sanctification, and being holy. These words typically mean "separate" or "being set apart." The biblical meaning of holiness and sanctification often has to do with separation.

A number of possible interpretations present themselves when we think of holiness as being separate or set apart. First, these biblical words might serve to indicate that God, the Creator of all, is far different from creatures. The difference may be that God is omnipresent, omniscient, or almighty. The difference may be that God has no beginning or end. Or the difference may be that God, as the holy one, has never sinned. Perhaps it is even sufficient to say that God is God, and we creatures are not! In all of these cases, God is other than (or *transcendent to*) creatures, which is the same as saying that God is radically set apart from us.

Second, when we talk about humans as separate or set apart, we may refer to identifying with a particular group. To be separate may involve choosing to associate with one community rather than another. In this case, the emphasis rests upon our own decisions. Sometimes, however, the biblical record places the emphasis upon God's choosing a particular people. In these cases, what is important is the idea that individuals or people are identified in contrast to others.

Third, being separated or set apart might also have to do with being designated or called to a particular task. Jesus was sanctified in this sense, because He said that the Father had called Him to certain purposes. Paul tells Timothy that Christians "will become special utensils, [sanctified] and useful to the owner of the house, ready for every good work" (2 Tim. 2:21). When we respond to God's call to do certain things or act in certain ways, we are holy in the sense of being set apart for a certain task.

Understanding holiness and sanctification as separation or being set apart in these various ways is important. But certain problems arise when we promote this meaning of holiness as the core notion of holiness.

While it is especially important to consider how God is different from us, holiness as God's transcendence does not account for why we should value holiness for humans. It does little to help us grasp how we ought to be Holiness people. It is impossible for us to "be holy as God is holy" if the way that God is holy is by being altogether different from us. As creatures, we cannot in this sense be like our Creator. We must seek another way to understand what must be meant by the passage in Leviticus that states, "You shall be holy, for I the LORD your God am holy" (19:2).

One problem with considering separation as the core idea—so as to associate with one group instead of another—is that sometimes no criteria are given for why one group is more worthy of our allegiance than another. Why choose to identify with one community rather than another? Simply being "different" isn't enough to motivate us for very long.

Another problem with separation as association with one group instead of another is that this notion fosters an exclusionary attitude of "us vs. them." There may be good reasons to be different from "them," but to set up an antagonistic or opposing relation with others without any reason other than the principle of being exclusive is ultimately unsatisfying. While relations in community are vital for the Christian life, we must find some reason or set of reasons to deem some communities more worthy of joining than others.

The idea that holiness has primarily to do with being called to a particular task vies powerfully for the label "the core notion of holiness." If we understand this call as coming from God, and if we believe that sanctification involves responding properly to that call, we have identified a crucial element of the holy life.

What prevents holiness as being called to a particular task from functioning as the core concept, however, is that in itself it doesn't go quite far enough. It doesn't tell us about the nature, characteristics, or quality of that call. To put the problem in the form of a question, "To what are we set apart?" Or to state it in the form of another question, "What is the character of the God who calls us to be set apart?"

Too many people today and throughout history have claimed that God has called them to commit acts of obvious evil. We've heard horrendous statements like "God told me to kill my baby" and "God has revealed to me that he approves of my extramarital sexual activity." The phrase "God called me to _____" can become a rubber stamp for the most ungodly behavior imaginable. To say that God calls us, therefore, tells us nothing about whether this call is good or evil, proper or improper, prosperous or decadent. While we may find no foolproof way to discern with certainty if God has asked us to do a particular task, we need something more specific than "God told me so."

Although the idea of holiness as being set apart is important, we must look elsewhere to find the core notion of holiness. It cannot unite the other legitimate, contributing concepts of holiness.

TOTAL COMMITMENT

There is another way to talk both about purity and being set apart as these relate to holiness. This way is to understand holiness as having to do with being consecrated, absolutely devoted, or totally committed.

The idea that humans are to commit themselves totally to God and thereby "have no other gods" is found in various forms throughout Scripture. Holiness leaders have understandably linked holiness, especially when using the phrase "entire sanctification," to the idea of total commitment.

The philosopher Søren Kierkegaard titled one of his books *Purity of the Heart Is to Will One Thing*, which illustrates how being pure can refer to total commitment. The pure in heart are those who single-mindedly devote themselves to someone or something. They have just one ultimate passion.

The way that being set apart relates to total commitment has to do with the answer to the question "Who sets us apart?" Biblical passages that speak of humans sanctifying themselves or choosing holiness typically have to do

with our decisions to be totally committed or absolutely
devoted. A biblical passage we looked at earlier illustrates
this. Peter instructs his readers to "sanctify Christ as Lord"
in their hearts (1 Pet. 3:15). In short, we are holy when we
commit ourselves wholly.

The problem with understanding holiness primarily in
terms of total commitment—purity of heart—has chiefly
to do with its vagueness. If the core of holiness has to do
with total commitment, one wonders, *Total commitment
to what?*

Even if we specify that we are talking about total commitment to God, we need to ask, "Whose view of God do
you mean? To what God are you totally committed?"
Many Muslims, Jews, and Hindus might be considered
part of the Holiness Movement in this broad sense of utter
devotion to God. In recent years, in fact, many Muslims
have shown their commitment—even to choosing certain
death—to a particular vision of God. Furthermore, the
various traditions of Christianity itself provide significantly different visions of the God to whom we should devote
ourselves. While being utterly devoted to God is vital, we
need some idea of the characteristics of that devotion.

In the end, the view of God we have becomes crucial.
This view largely determines what we should expect from
holy people. So while it is important to understand holiness as having to do with total commitment, this understanding cannot itself serve as the core notion of holiness.
More work needs to be done to describe the God to whom
we should be devoted.

BEING PERFECT

We conclude this chapter with a final way that Christians throughout the centuries have understood holiness. Following the command that Jesus gave, "Be perfect, therefore, as your heavenly Father is perfect" (Matt. 5:48), Christians have equated being holy with being perfect.

The Holiness Movement, beginning about 300 years ago with John Wesley, has become well known—some would say notorious—for talking about perfection in this life. Clarifying in what ways one can be called "perfect" has been an ongoing and perhaps often unsuccessful project.

The main problem with equating holiness with perfection has to do with the various meanings of perfection. For instance, some equate perfection with lack of change. This notion of perfection would seem to apply only to God's eternal nature. If God were perfect in this way, God could change only for the worse. If one is perfect in this sense, it seems impossible to change for the better. If we use holiness to mean lack of change, it is ridiculous to think that constantly changing creatures like ourselves could be perfect even as our Father in heaven is perfect.

Others use perfection in the sense made famous by Aristotle. This involves being fit for or accomplishing a specific purpose. In this sense, almost anything can be perfect so long as it fulfills its purpose. Cups are holy if they fulfill their purpose of holding water. Atheists can be holy if we define perfection in this way, so long as they fulfill their purpose as atheists. Aristotle's idea of perfection holds promise for understanding holiness, but it requires an answer to the question "What is our purpose?"

Still others speak of perfection in the sense of never sinning. To be perfect is never to have sinned. Because only God is morally perfect in this sense, it is difficult to see how this sense of perfection can be meaningfully applied to humans. After all, we have all sinned (Rom. 3:23).

Some meanings of perfection are helpful for understanding holiness. We will address these later in the book. But like the other concepts of holiness in this chapter, holiness as perfection—at least without further explanation—best serves as a contributory rather than core notion.

We have looked at various understandings of holiness and sanctification that are prominent in the Bible. In this process, we concluded that these understandings were helpful and important. But we also concluded that none could serve well as the core notion of holiness. All were water, air, fire, and dirt.

We will consider these contributing notions of holiness again in the final chapter. Now we turn to one more notion of holiness. We suggest that it can serve as the core.

QUESTIONS TO STIMULATE DISCUSSION

1. Are you surprised to find that the words "holy," "holiness," and "sanctification" have diverse meanings in the Bible? How might you account for this diversity?

2. Which meanings of holiness do you recall hearing emphasized by Christians you have known?

3. What has been your experience with understanding holiness as following rules and regulations? Do you find this helpful?

4. Do you think it is possible for people to be entirely pure? Do you find it helpful to think of holiness as personal purity? Why or why not?

5. What do you think of understanding holiness as total commitment? In what ways is this understanding helpful or unhelpful?

6. In what ways do you find holiness as being set apart valuable or not valuable?

7. Can you be perfect in any sense? How do you feel about the call to be perfect? Is holiness best understood in terms of Christian perfection?

FOR DEEPER STUDY

Bassett, Paul. *Holiness Teachings: New Testament Times to John Wesley.* Kansas City: Beacon Hill Press of Kansas City, 1997.

———. "Jesus' Call to Perfection (Matt. 5:48)." *Biblical Resources for Holiness Preaching: From Text to Sermon.* Vol. 2, edited by H. Ray Dunning. Kansas City: Beacon Hill Press of Kansas City, 1993.

Boone, Dan. "Follow-through (Rom. 12:1-2)." In *Biblical Resources for Holiness Preaching: From Text to Sermon.* Vol. 1, edited by H. Ray Dunning and Neil B. Wiseman. Kansas City: Beacon Hill Press of Kansas City, 1993.

Brannon, Wilbur. "Holiness—a Resurrection Possibility (Acts 26:16-18)." In *Biblical Resources for Holiness Preaching: From Text to Sermon.* Vol. 1, edited by H. Ray Dunning and Neil B. Wiseman. Kansas City: Beacon Hill Press of Kansas City, 1993.

Branson, Robert D. "Holiness: The Law Written Within (Jer. 31:31-34)." In *Biblical Resources for Holiness Preaching: From Text to Sermon.* Vol. 2, edited by H. Ray Dunning. Kansas City: Beacon Hill Press of Kansas City, 1993.

Bratcher, Dennis. "Psalm 51 and the Language of Transformation: A Biblical Perspective on Holiness." <http://www.cresourcei.org/psa51.html>.

Brower, Kent. "Purity of Heart (Matt. 5:8)." In *Biblical Resources for Holiness Preaching: From Text to Sermon.* Vol. 2, edited by H. Ray Dunning. Kansas City: Beacon Hill Press of Kansas City, 1993.

Bundy, David. "Visions of Sanctification." *Wesleyan Theological Journal.* 39:1 (spring 2004).

Carver, Frank G. "The Sacrifice that Sanctifies (Heb. 10:11-18)." In *Biblical Resources for Holiness Preaching: From Text to Sermon.* Vol. 2, edited by H. Ray Dunning. Kansas City: Beacon Hill Press of Kansas City, 1993.

———. "Through and Through Sanctification (1 Thess. 5:23-24)." In *Biblical Resources for Holiness Preaching: From Text to Sermon.* Vol. 2, edited by H. Ray Dunning. Kansas City: Beacon Hill Press of Kansas City, 1993.

Cauthron, Hal A. "Holiness—a Matter of Dying (Gal. 2:20)." In *Biblical Resources for Holiness Preaching: From Text to Sermon*. Vol. 1, edited by H. Ray Dunning and Neil B. Wiseman. Kansas City: Beacon Hill Press of Kansas City, 1993.

———. "The Rest of Faith (Heb. 4:9-10)." In *Biblical Resources for Holiness Preaching: From Text to Sermon*. Vol. 2, edited by H. Ray Dunning. Kansas City: Beacon Hill Press of Kansas City, 1993.

Cowles, C. S. "Holiness as Freedom from Sin (1 John 2:1-14)." In *Biblical Resources for Holiness Preaching: From Text to Sermon*. Vol. 1, edited by H. Ray Dunning and Neil B. Wiseman. Kansas City: Beacon Hill Press of Kansas City, 1993.

Dunnington, Don. "Holiness and the Spirit-filled Life (Eph. 5:15-21)." In *Biblical Resources for Holiness Preaching: From Text to Sermon*. Vol. 2, edited by H. Ray Dunning. Kansas City: Beacon Hill Press of Kansas City, 1993.

Edlin, James O., "Hostility to Hospitality Through Holiness (2 Cor. 6:14 —7:1)." In *Biblical Resources for Holiness Preaching: From Text to Sermon*. Vol. 2, edited by H. Ray Dunning. Kansas City: Beacon Hill Press of Kansas City, 1993.

Greathouse, William M. *Wholeness in Christ: Toward a Biblical Theology of Holiness*. Kansas City: Beacon Hill Press of Kansas City, 1968.

Green, Stephen D. "Newness of Life (Rom. 6:1-14)." In *Biblical Resources for Holiness Preaching: From Text to Sermon*. Vol. 2, edited by H. Ray Dunning. Kansas City: Beacon Hill Press of Kansas City, 1993.

———. "An Old Testament Call to Perfection (Gen. 17:1)." In *Biblical Resources for Holiness Preaching: From Text to Sermon*. Vol. 1, edited by H. Ray Dunning and Neil B. Wiseman. Kansas City: Beacon Hill Press of Kansas City, 1993.

Green, Timothy. "A New Heart—to the Glory of God! (Ezek. 36:22-28)." In *Biblical Resources for Holiness Preaching: From Text to Sermon*. Vol. 2, edited by H. Ray Dunning. Kansas City: Beacon Hill Press of Kansas City, 1993.

Hahn, Roger L. "Jesus' Prayer for Our Holiness." In *Biblical Resources for Holiness Preaching: From Text to Sermon*. Vol. 2, edited by H. Ray Dunning. Kansas City: Beacon Hill Press of Kansas City, 1993.

————. "Law and the Spirit (Rom. 8:1-4)." In *Biblical Resources for Holiness Preaching: From Text to Sermon*. Vol. 1, edited by H. Ray Dunning and Neil B. Wiseman. Kansas City: Beacon Hill Press of Kansas City, 1993.

Howard, Richard. "Two Ways to Live (Gal. 5:16-25)." In *Biblical Resources for Holiness Preaching: From Text to Sermon*. Vol. 2, edited by H. Ray Dunning. Kansas City: Beacon Hill Press of Kansas City, 1993.

Leadingham, Everett, ed. *A Hunger for God: What the Bible Really Says About Holiness*. Kansas City: Beacon Hill Press of Kansas City, 2002.

Lyons, George. *Holiness in Everyday Life*. Kansas City: Beacon Hill Press of Kansas City, 1992.

————. "Holiness in God's Eternal Plan of Redemption (Eph. 1:3-14)." In *Biblical Resources for Holiness Preaching: From Text to Sermon*. Vol. 2, edited by H. Ray Dunning. Kansas City: Beacon Hill Press of Kansas City, 1993.

————. "Modeling the Holiness Ethos: A Study Based on First Thessalonians." *Wesleyan Theological Journal* 30:1 (spring 1995).

McCant, Jerry W. "Holiness as an Ethical Life-style (1 John 2:28—3:3)." In *Biblical Resources for Holiness Preaching: From Text to Sermon*. Vol. 2, edited by H. Ray Dunning. Kansas City: Beacon Hill Press of Kansas City, 1993.

McCullough, Melvin. "Holiness as Inner Resource (Eph. 3:14-19)." In *Biblical Resources for Holiness Preaching: From Text to Sermon*. Vol. 1, edited by H. Ray Dunning and Neil B. Wiseman. Kansas City: Beacon Hill Press of Kansas City, 1993.

Neilson, John M. "Holiness—an Atonement Provision (Heb. 13:12)." In *Biblical Resources for Holiness Preaching: From Text to Sermon*. Vol. 1, edited by H. Ray Dunning and Neil B. Wiseman. Kansas City: Beacon Hill Press of Kansas City, 1993.

Peterson, Bruce. "Paul's Prayer for the Philippian Church (Rom. 13:8)." In *Biblical Resources for Holiness Preaching: From Text to Sermon*. Vol. 1, edited by H. Ray Dunning and Neil B. Wiseman. Kansas City: Beacon Hill Press of Kansas City, 1993.

Phillips, Thomas E. "Reading Theory and Biblical Interpretation." *Wesleyan Theological Journal* 35:2 (fall 2000).

"Reminting Christian Holiness." Website at <www.holiness.nazarene. ac.uk>.

Serrão, C. Jeanne Orjala. *Holiness and Sexual Ethics in Paul: An Analysis of the Use of Social Sciences in the Study of the New Testament.* Ann Arbor, Mich.: UMI Microform 9703842, 1996.

Smith, Robert K. "Keeping the Temple Clean (2 Cor. 6:14—7:1)." In *Biblical Resources for Holiness Preaching: From Text to Sermon.* Vol. 1, edited by H. Ray Dunning and Neil B. Wiseman. Kansas City: Beacon Hill Press of Kansas City, 1993.

Spross, Daniel. "Holiness in the Pastor Epistles (1 and 2 Tim.; Titus)." In *Biblical Resources for Holiness Preaching: From Text to Sermon.* Vol. 1, edited by H. Ray Dunning and Neil B. Wiseman. Kansas City: Beacon Hill Press of Kansas City, 1993.

Strawn, Brent A. "Leviticus 19:1-2, 9-18." In *The Lectionary Commentary: Theological Exegesis for Sunday's Texts, The First Readings: The Old Testament and Acts.* Edited by Roger E. Van Harn. Grand Rapids: Wm. B. Eerdmans Publishing Co., 2001.

———. "The X-Factor: Revisioning Biblical Holiness." *Asbury Theological Journal* 54:2 (fall 1999).

Thorsen, Don. *The Wesleyan Quadrilateral.* Grand Rapids: Zondervan Publishing House, 1990.

Tracy, Wesley D. "The Cleansing Blood of Jesus (1 John 1:5—2:2)." In *Biblical Resources for Holiness Preaching: From Text to Sermon.* Vol. 2, edited by H. Ray Dunning. Kansas City: Beacon Hill Press of Kansas City, 1993.

———. "Holiness 101." In *Holiness 101: Exploring This Transforming Journey.* Kansas City: Beacon Hill Press of Kansas City, 2003.

Varughese, Alex. "Holiness and Pastoral Responsibility (Titus 2:11-14)." In *Biblical Resources for Holiness Preaching: From Text to Sermon.* Vol. 1, edited by H. Ray Dunning and Neil B. Wiseman. Kansas City: Beacon Hill Press of Kansas City, 1993.

———. "Holiness and Sexual Purity (1 Thess. 4:1-8)." In *Biblical Resources for Holiness Preaching: From Text to Sermon.* Vol. 2, edited by H. Ray Dunning. Kansas City: Beacon Hill Press of Kansas City, 1993.

Wall, Robert. "Purity and Power According to the Acts of the Apostles." *Wesleyan Theological Journal* 34:1 (spring 1999).

Wiseman, Neil B. "Jesus' Baptism with the Holy Spirit." In *Biblical Resources for Holiness Preaching: From Text to Sermon.* Vol. 1, edited by H. Ray Dunning and Neil B. Wiseman. Kansas City: Beacon Hill Press of Kansas City, 1993.

Wynkoop, Mildred Bangs. *A Theology of Love: The Dynamic of Wesleyanism.* Kansas City: Beacon Hill Press of Kansas City, 1972.

3
Adventures in Love

Søren Kierkegaard was a 19th-century Danish philosopher whose ideas have had a lasting influence in the Western world. As a young man, Kierkegaard wrote these words in his journal: "I want a truth for which I can live and die."

We also want a truth for which we can live and die. Without it, life has no ultimate meaning. Without this truth, we have no purpose, no significant values, and no hope. We want a truth that gives us a reason to exist.

Is holiness that truth? As we have presented it thus far, it might be difficult to convince us that it is. Although we noted the importance of several meanings of holiness, we determined that they were contributory notions. By themselves, each presented problems. None alone could serve as the core notion of holiness.

There is yet another meaning of holiness and sanctification. We mentioned it briefly in the previous chapter. This meaning of holiness has to do with *love*.

In this chapter, we propose that love functions well as

the core notion of holiness. Love provides the foundation and framework for faith. God's love for us and our love in return, as well as our love for our neighbors and ourselves, resides at the core of Christianity. Love provides holiness with the foundation it needs to flourish as the theological distinctive of the Holiness tradition.

And love is a truth for which we can live and die.

LOVE AS THE CORE OF HOLINESS

Several passages in the Bible suggest that love is the core of holiness. We listed a few in the previous chapter. For instance, Paul blesses his readers by saying, "May the Lord make you increase and abound in love for one another and for all, just as we abound in love for you. And may he so strengthen your hearts in holiness" (1 Thess. 3:12-13).

The argument that love serves well as the core of holiness, however, does not rely primarily upon biblical passages showing an essential relationship between the two. Instead, the argument appeals to the most fundamental themes of the Bible. Only in appealing to these themes can we account for the diverse biblical witness. And only then can we identify an integrative and inclusive notion of holiness.

To find the core themes of Christianity, we begin with the doctrine of God. This means that we discover the core meaning of holiness by asking who God is. Such an approach makes sense if we want to follow God's instructions found in both Leviticus and 1 Peter: "You shall be holy, for I the Lord your God am holy." To discover what holiness is, we need to ponder the nature and activity of God.

We believe that the most fundamental claim about who God is—the very heart of an adequate doctrine of God—derives from this simple three-word sentence: "God is love."

Love is the Christian centerpiece and foundation for the most adequate descriptions of God. Although God has other attributes, none seem as central to the biblical witness and to Christianity. God's essence is love, and God acts lovingly out of that essence.

"God is love," writes John, "and those who abide in love abide in God, and God abides in them" (1 John 4:16). "For God so loved the world . . ." begins perhaps the most well-known verse from the Bible, John 3:16. From Genesis to Revelation, the story of God revolves around love.

The Great Commandments provide basic instructions for how we ought to act. Mark records them this way: "You shall love the Lord your God with all your heart, and with all your soul, and with all your mind, and with all your strength" (Mark 12:30). And the second is like the first: "You shall love your neighbor as yourself." Jesus adds, "There is no commandment greater than these" (v. 31). Paul echoes these words by writing that "the one who loves another has fulfilled the law" (Rom. 13:8).

When we consider the scriptural context of Jesus' instructions to His disciples to "be perfect, therefore, as your heavenly Father is perfect" (Matt. 5:48), it becomes clear that God's love provides the key to understanding holiness. This instruction in Matthew's Gospel is interchangeable with Luke's version of that same verse: "Be merciful, just as your Father is merciful" (Luke 6:36). Or, as Paul puts it, "Be imitators of God, as beloved children, and live in love as Christ loved us" (Eph. 5:1-2).

The core meaning of holiness derives from divine love. When we look at all the concepts of holiness described in the last chapter, we find that love integrates their positive meanings.

To be holy is to love—to love God, neighbors, and God's creation, including ourselves. We are holy as God is holy when we love as God loves. While other notions of holiness contribute something valuable to our general understanding, the core meaning of holiness is love.

WHAT IS LOVE?

"Love" is perhaps the most used and yet least understood of all English words. It is a notoriously ambiguous weasel-word. The claim that love is the core of holiness, therefore, requires further explanation.

Many ideas about love exist. Here are just a few:

Love is a kind of warfare.
—Ovid

Love ain't nothin' but sex misspelled.
—Harlan Ellison

Love is a never-ending feeling.
—Adeil Prince

Love makes the world go 'round.
—Various

Love is just another four-letter word.
—Tennessee Williams

Love kills.

—Sid Vicious

Love means never having to say you're sorry.

—*Love Story*

Love is a perky elf dancing a merry little jig, and then he suddenly turns on you with a miniature machine gun.

—Matt Groening

When Christians use the word "love," they generally mean something quite different from what is described in these quotations. Christians also frequently use the word to mean something other than dating, romance, or sex. When talking about love for God, the Christian means something different than love for chocolate cake. And Christians typically don't equate love with extreme permissiveness, wimpiness, or a laid-back attitude. For Christians, love doesn't mean "anything goes."

Let's begin to explain what we mean by love with a somewhat technical definition. This definition is crucial if we are to talk meaningfully about love as the core of holiness. Following our definition of love, we will briefly explain its components.

Definition: To love is to act intentionally, in response to God and others, to promote well-being. To say the same thing in other words, to love is to respond to the inspiration of others—especially God—and by that response effect genuine flourishing.

Let's break this definition into pieces for analysis. First, to love is to act. Love is a verb; love is something you do.

These actions may be expressed with members of our bodies, or we may act only by thinking. Furthermore, loving actions are intentional, which means that they are deliberate. While unintended actions may produce something good, only those that are intentional should be considered loving.

Intentional actions contain decisions with some degree of freedom as to what can be decided. This means that love has an intellectual dimension, even if the intellect does not always play a major role in the act of love. And it means that love cannot be coerced. Some modicum of freedom is present when we choose love.

Second, love involves response. One might say that response involves being affected by, sympathizing with, or, if you prefer, empathizing with others. Because we are all relational beings, and each moment of our lives begins with the influence of others, love involves response. Love arises in the give-and-take of life.

Love as response means that love usually involves some degree of emotion. Love may be charged with high emotions, or a love response may barely register on the sentiment scale. Love may be warm and fuzzy, or it may be cool and highly calculating. Love entails, as psychologists might put it, a degree of affect.

God is the most important influence for our love. We are able to love because we respond to—we sympathize with—God's initiating influence. Or, as John says it, "We love because he first loved us" (1 John 4:19). Paul puts it this way: we love because God first poured love into our

hearts, and divine action makes creaturely love possible
(Rom. 5:5). We depend upon God's love—expressed in relationship to us—so that we might love in response.

Well-being is the third element in our definition that
needs further explanation. Perhaps the most common
synonym for well-being is "happiness." Love generates
happiness. Many philosophers prefer the word "flourishing" to happiness or well-being, but the same idea is inherent in all three. It is also present in the rich Hebraic
word *shalom.*

Biblical translators use several words to capture the
idea of well-being. In addition to "happy" and "good," one
of the most common is "blessed." To experience God's
blessing is to enjoy the well-being that love produces. And
Jesus speaks of well-being when he says that He came
"that they may have life and have it abundantly" (John
10:10). Love breeds abundant life.

We use the phrase "well-being" when describing love,
because we think that it suggests to contemporary people
a fuller representation of the good that love promotes.
When we think of well-being, we think of its many facets,
including its social, emotional, physical, economic, political, mental, and even ecological dimensions. Well-being is
a word that many social scientists, such as psychologists
and health-care providers, use to talk about full-bodied
happiness.

To say that love promotes well-being is also to suggest
that love—and therefore holiness—promotes wholeness.
The Christian life involves a kind of therapy, as God works
in the world to heal the sin-sick and diseased. And we im-

itate God's love when we live in ways that bring abundant life to the ill and injured in all creation. Holiness engenders wholeness.

WHAT FORMS DOES LOVE TAKE?

Now that we've defined love as intentional response to others—especially God—that promotes well-being, we need to look at some concrete examples of love. Having a definition is important, but we also want to identify some ways that love might be expressed.

Some of the most common expressions of love are actions such as forgiving, offering words of encouragement, donating time or money, displaying self-control, showing humility, showing trust, showing respect, showing compassion, telling the truth, being patient, liberating the captive and oppressed, and being kind.

We may not think even the expressions just listed are specific enough. To be more specific, we may say that writing a conciliatory letter to an offended friend is an act of love. A specific act of love may involve sending money to a relief organization so that underprivileged children might be fed and educated. To act lovingly may mean serving in one's community. Of course, a complete list of loving actions would be extremely long. The preceding list is like the tip of an iceberg.

French philosopher La Rochefoucould once wisely said, "There is only one kind of love, but there are a thousand different versions." He should have said *several* thousand different versions.

The actions listed above, however, are not *always* expressions of love. For instance, donating money is not always an act that promotes well-being. Money can be donated to people or organizations that cause harm. Encouraging others may not always be a loving action. After all, some people encourage their associates to commit evil acts. And at some point even the act of being patient may become an act of enabling that fosters injustice.

It is one's context that largely decides which acts are loving and which are not. What form love should take depends upon a variety of factors to which we intentionally respond to God and others as we seek to promote abundant life. To say this in a relational way, the relations we have with others, especially our relation with God, largely determine what counts as love in any particular moment.

To say that one's context largely decides what love requires is not an affirmation of a situational ethic in which morality is relative. We would do well to reject moral relativism; it is a dead-end street. Instead, God is the omnipresent One—we might say the omnicontextual One—and God calls us to love in specific ways in whatever context we find ourselves. The context largely determines what counts as loving, because God is part of every context. Only the God whose character never changes and who relates to all creation knows best how to promote abundant life for all creatures in all circumstances.

Consider the claim that love requires us to give to those who ask of us. Is giving to others always the loving thing to do? When we receive e-mails from some unknown gentleman in a far-off country asking us to transfer funds from our bank account, does love require that we give the money? Most of the time love does not require this transfer, and the context helps us realize that God does not call us to be victims of what is a likely scam.

Or consider the claim that love demands that spouses never part. The vast majority of the time, love requires spouses to honor their pledge to remain together "until death do us part." But when one spouse physically abuses another such that the abused one's life is in danger, God's call to love may mean separation, at least for a time. Sometimes our choices are between bad and worse. God calls us to promote well-being to the extent possible in any context, even the messiest ones.

The God who is active in every context desires to bless all creation with flourishing. The fact that God loves is true in any and every context. *How* God decides to love depends upon the individuals and variables in each context. The request that our love take a particular form comes from God, and God is fully aware of how well-being might best be promoted in any particular context.

The discussion of context leads us to consider other ways to talk about the forms that love takes. Many refer to a variety of ancient Greek words to talk about different types. The most common Greek love-words are *agape*, *eros*, and *philia*. But it is difficult to know exactly what each word means.

Unfortunately, many Christians have been told that the biblical authors reserve the word *agape* only for talking about God's unconditional love. This is simply not true.

Like the various meanings of holiness and sanctification noted earlier, biblical writers use *agape* in a variety of ways, apparently intending a variety of meanings.

Just because biblical authors use *agape* in a variety of ways does not mean that the word is not useful. Those who use *agape* today, however, need to define well what they mean. And the more adequate definitions will correspond well with dominant biblical themes.

We define *agape* as acting to promote well-being when responding to actions that cause ill-being. Or to use the words of Scripture, *agape* repays evil with good. Paul uses *agape* in this general way when he writes, "God proves his love for us in that while we still were sinners Christ died for us" (Rom. 5:8).

God calls us to express *agape*. Evil should elicit in us the kind of response it elicits in God: *agape*. Just as God responds to sin by loving in ways that offer abundant life, so we must respond in love to those who sin against us by acting in ways that promote abundant life. We are to love our enemies. Such *agape* is expressed by the apostle Paul's instructions to "bless those who persecute you; bless and do not curse them" (Rom. 12:14). If we love in this way, we will be holy as God is holy.

Sometimes God does not call us to *agape*. Sometimes God calls us to love that which is valuable, beautiful, or desirable. The Greek word *eros* conveys this love response. We define *eros* as acting to promote well-being by affirming and enjoying what is valuable.

Some Christian theological traditions have so emphasized the sinfulness of creatures that they cannot account for the fact that God created the world and called it good. These traditions cannot account for passages of Scripture that speak of God's being pleased, happy, and proud of what we have done. They allow no place for divine *eros*.

And some Christian theological traditions ignore biblical references to the appropriateness of *philia*. *Philia* is love that promotes well-being by seeking to establish deeper bonds of cooperative friendship. Although the Bible clearly talks about God's enjoying friendship with us, some Christians characterize God as aloof and unaffected by the give-and-receive of friendship. When God is thought not capable of friendship, God is typically not considered relational.

We believe that God expresses all three types of love: *agape, eros,* and *philia*. God's action arsenal contains a variety of love-types. We might say that God's love is full-orbed—expressing each of the three love-types—rather than half-baked.

God responds to us in just the right way. When we sin, God responds by acting in ways that call us to wholeness. When we love, God responds in love like a proud parent who enjoys the beauty and worth of what faithful children have done and who they are. And God always acts to deepen and develop an ongoing heritage of enriching friendship.

If we are to follow Paul's instructions to "be imitators of God . . . and live in love, as Christ loved us" (Eph. 5:1-2), and if we are to be holy because our Lord God is holy, our love ought also be full-orbed. Depending on the circumstances, this may mean turning the other cheek, taking pleasure in and enhancing the beauty of creation, or establishing the bonds of community. When we express *agape, eros,* and/or *philia* in the proper contexts, we are holy as God is holy.

THE ADVENTURE OF RELATIONAL HOLINESS

Throughout this chapter we have talked about the importance of one's context and relationships, especially with God, for determining what love requires. This idea undergirds relational holiness. But we need to be clearer about the characteristics of relational holiness.

Perhaps the best historical link to relational holiness is a doctrine found in the very theological tradition that sustains holiness theology: Wesleyanism. According to it, God "walks ahead of us," enabling us to choose salvation freely. The technical label for this doctrine, briefly mentioned in our discussion of postmodernism, is "prevenient grace." God's prevenient grace sets the context for our responses, because God acts first to offer us abundant life.

In terms of relational holiness, we say that God relates to us by acting first in every moment to provide us with opportunities for action. Those opportunities arise out of God's own actions, the actions of others, and our own previous actions. The relations we have with God and others set the context for each moment of our lives.

God's moment-by-moment calls require our response. God calls us to love according to the multilayered relations in which we live. Among all possible actions, God encourages us to choose that which promotes well-being.

God makes it possible for us to respond freely and thereby act in one way instead of another.

When we choose the best to which God calls in any particular moment, we act in holiness. In that moment, we are "perfect . . . as [our] heavenly Father is perfect" (Matt. 5:48). In that moment, we love. Responding appropriately to God's prevenient call in any particular moment is a response of love.

Relational holiness entails our responding appropriately to God's call to love in a particular way, at a particular time, and in a particular situation. The opportunity for love is present in every moment. As Mother Teresa put it, "Love is a fruit in season at all times, and within the reach of every hand." In most moments, the opportunities for love will be fairly mundane. But in others, God offers us the chance to love in ways that radically affect our world and ourselves.

Relational holiness as our moment-by-moment response to God's love provides a unique—and we think decidedly biblical—view of the Christian life. We might think of the ongoing life of relational holiness as an adventure. Let's call it the "Adventure Model" of holiness.

According to the Adventure Model, each traveler sets out on an open-ended and largely unplanned adventure. The journey will inevitably include challenges, but the traveler will also encounter opportunities for great joy.

An ever-present and constantly communicating Guide calls out to the adventurer each step of the way. Prior to each step, the Guide presents the adventurer with a number of options. Without the Guide's initiating prompting, the adventurer would be lost.

Some options that the Guide presents, if chosen, produce happiness and wholeness. Other options, if chosen, lead to unjustified suffering and evil. The negative actions of others on the journey produce these negative options to our adventurer. The Guide can be trusted to show the adventurer the best paths to take.

The Guide encourages the adventurer to take the step that causes happiness and wholeness. In other words, travelers are called to love. The Guide walks alongside each adventurer and acts first to encourage him or her to choose what is loving. The Guide awaits the adventurer's free response to the options at hand.

Occasionally, the adventurer "hears" the Guide's tutoring rather clearly. But most of the time, the adventurer hears only a still, small Voice. Whether the Guide's instruction seems clear or faint, the adventurer is responsible to respond appropriately.

Although the adventurer has the help of a Guide, other help is also available on this journey. No adventurer walks alone. Other adventurers form a community of fellow-travelers. In fact, we might call these travelers "adventurers-in-community." Supportive adventurers provide help to one another while drawing upon the collected wisdom of those who have earlier walked similar paths. We might call it social holiness.   *Is this what Wesley called Soc. Hol?*

Along the way, our adventurers-in-community discover that various habits, resources, and customs can make the journey better for everyone involved. The Guide often uses these habits, resources, and customs to encourage these wayfarers. In fact, our adventurers typically come to rely upon these helpful means so much that they cannot imagine how to navigate successfully without them.

This adventure in which the Guide calls and the travelers respond continues on and on. Someday the terrain will be significantly different, because obstacles that lead the travelers astray will no longer exist. While the thought of that day brings some comfort, the greatest comfort comes in knowing that the Guide walks beside and makes the first move to inspire each step of the adventure. Adventurers can live this life with meaning and zest, knowing that appropriate responses make the journey better for everyone.

The Adventure Model of holiness differs significantly from what might be called the "Slide Scenario" of holiness. The Slide Scenario involves a never-ending cycle of climbing up only to slip back.

In the Slide Scenario, the climber slowly ascends the face of the slide rather than scaling the stairs. This rise up the slide's face is possible only as the climber follows various rules, avoids wrongdoing, and remains obedient. The longer one avoids sin, the higher one climbs the slide.

Almost inevitably, however, the climber loses footing. Temptation prevails, and sin is committed. A misstep erases all the progress that had been made. The climber slips and slides all the way back to the bottom.

The fall plunges the climber to the playground sand. And no one knows if the courage to climb again will return. Like the mythical Sisyphus, who is cursed to push a rock up a mountain only to have it roll back down, the process of climbing and falling continues endlessly. It's a game of Chutes and Ladders that can never be won.

There are many differences between the Adventure Model and the Slide Scenario. The adventurer has a Guide who calls and to whom a response is given. The adventurer relies upon that Guide, because no adventurer is able to pull himself or herself up by his or her own bootstraps. And the Guide is faithful to do what is best according to the path the adventurer takes.

The adventurer also travels with companions and uses habits, resources, and customs that help on the journey. A misstep does not return the adventurer back to the journey's beginning. Rather, the Guide offers new options in each moment based upon the adventurer's previous actions and varying relations. Like a "choose-your-own-adventure" book, every step provides new opportunities and opens new paths.

We believe that the Adventure Model is more faithful to the dominant themes of the Bible. It emphasizes the all-important relations we have with God while also stressing the importance of our relations with others. We also believe that relational holiness as depicted in the Adventure Model makes sense in the postmodern world.

The ongoing life of loving God, others, and God's creation, including ourselves, is the life of holiness. And today we need this adventure in holiness, understood in terms of relational love, more than ever.

QUESTIONS TO STIMULATE DISCUSSION

1. The authors say that to be holy is to love, and that we are holy as God is holy when we love as God loves. What do you think of this understanding of holiness?

2. To love is to act intentionally, in response to God and others, to promote well-being. After hearing an explanation of this love definition, what do you think of it?

3. How might relations with others—God, humans, and even nonhumans—affect what love requires?

4. What do you think it means to say that love promotes well-being?

5. Love is said to take a variety of types (*agape, eros, philia*), and God is said to express each of them. What are some advantages in claiming that God expresses a variety of loves?

6. In what ways do you think God expresses *eros* and *philia*? What are examples of times that we should express these loves?

7. What are the main points of both the Slide Scenario and Adventure Model of holiness? Do you find these metaphors helpful in explaining two different philosophies of holiness?

FOR DEEPER STUDY

Bassett, Paul. "Holiness as Love in Relation to Others (Rom. 13:8)." In *Biblical Resources for Holiness Preaching: From Text to Sermon*. Vol. 1, edited by H. Ray Dunning and Neil B. Wiseman. Kansas City: Beacon Hill Press of Kansas City, 1993.

Braaten, Laurie J. "Love." In *Eerdmans Dictionary of the Bible*. Edited by David Noel Freedman. Grand Rapids: Wm. B. Eerdmans Publishing Co., 2000.

Callen, Barry L. *God as Loving Grace*. Nappanee, Ind.: Evangel Publishing House, 1996.

Daniels, Scott T. "Religious Ethics." In *Philosophy of Religion: Introductory Essays*. Edited by Thomas Jay Oord. Kansas City: Beacon Hill Press of Kansas City, 2003.

Dunning, H. Ray. *Grace, Faith, and Holiness: A Wesleyan Systematic Theology*. Kansas City: Beacon Hill Press of Kansas City, 1988.

Dunnington, Don W. "Holiness as Love of God." In *Biblical Resources for Holiness Preaching: From Text to Sermon*. Vol. 1, edited by H. Ray Dunning and Neil B. Wiseman. Kansas City: Beacon Hill Press of Kansas City, 1993.

Greathouse, William. *Love Made Perfect: Foundations for the Holy Life*. Kansas City: Beacon Hill Press of Kansas City, 1997.

Johnson, W. Stanley. "Christian Perfection as Love for God." *Wesleyan Theological Journal* 18:1 (spring 1983).

Knight, John A. *All Loves Excelling: Proclaiming Our Wesleyan Message*. Kansas City: Beacon Hill Press of Kansas City, 1995.

Lee, Bernard. *The Becoming of the Church: A Process Theology of the Structure of Christian Experience*. New York: Paulist Press, 1974.

Lodahl, Michael E. "And He Felt Compassion." In *Embodied Holiness: Toward a Corporate Theology of Spiritual Growth*. Edited by Samuel M. Powell and Michael E. Lodahl. Downers Grove, Ill.: InterVarsity Press, 1999.

———. "Divine Holiness." In *Philosophy of Religion: Introductory Essays*. Kansas City: Beacon Hill Press of Kansas City, 2003.

———. *God of Nature and of Grace: Reading the World in a Wesleyan Way*. Nashville: Kingswood Press, 2003.

————. *The Story of God: Wesleyan Theology and Biblical Narrative.* Kansas City: Beacon Hill Press of Kansas City, 1994.

Maddox, Randy L. *Responsible Grace: John Wesley's Practical Theology.* Nashville: Kingswood Press, 1994.

McCumber, W. E. "The Greatest Commandment (Mark 12:28-34)." In *Biblical Resources for Holiness Preaching: From Text to Sermon.* Vol. 2, edited by H. Ray Dunning. Kansas City: Beacon Hill Press of Kansas City, 1993.

Oord, Thomas Jay. "Agape, Altruism, and Well-Being: Full-Orbed Love for the Science and Religion Love Dialogue." *Contemporary Philosophy: Philosophic Research, Analysis and Resolution* 24:1 & 2 (January-February & March-April 2002).

————. "Divine Love." In *Philosophy of Religion: Introductory Essays.* Edited by Thomas Jay Oord. Kansas City: Beacon Hill Press of Kansas City, 2003.

————. *Science of Love: The Wisdom of Well-Being.* Philadelphia: Templeton Press, 2004.

Pinnock, Clark, et al. *The Openness of God: A Biblical Challenge to the Traditional Understanding of God.* Downers Grove, Ill.: InterVarsity Press, 1994.

Post, Stephen G. *Unlimited Love: Altruism, Compassion, Service.* Philadelphia: Templeton Press, 2003.

Stone, Bryan P. "The Spirit and the Holy Life." *Quarterly Review* 21:2 (summer 2001).

Suchocki, Marjorie Hewitt. *The Fall to Violence: Original Sin in Relational Theology.* New York: Continuum Press, 1995.

Swanson, Dwight. "Part 40: Sin and Love in 1 John." <holiness.nazarene .ac.uk/articles.php?n=40>.

Taylor, Richard S. "The Abiding Relevance of Divine Love." *Wesleyan Theological Journal* 2:1 (spring 1967).

Tink, Fletcher L. "Love in Three Ventricles" <www.nazcompassion.org>.

Truesdale, Al and Bonnie Perry. *A Dangerous Hope: Encountering the God of Grace.* Kansas City: Beacon Hill Press of Kansas City, 1998.

Wynkoop, Mildred Bangs. *A Theology of Love: The Dynamic of Wesleyanism.* Kansas City: Beacon Hill Press of Kansas City, 1972.

4
Sharing in the Love of the Trinity

We suggested in the previous chapter that the deceptively simple claim that "God is love" (1 John 4:8, 16) resides at the center of a Christian understanding of divine holiness. In this chapter we explore this fundamental statement even further. We ask again how this three-word phrase sheds light on what it means to be holy.

The Christian leader who perhaps thought most deeply about holiness was John Wesley. Wesley argued that the statement "God is love" is the single most important description of God in all of Scripture. While this simple phrase typifies the biblical testimony as a whole regarding God's identity and character, it is worth noting that "God is love" is found specifically in the New Testament letter of 1 John. In our efforts to unpack the meaning of "God is love," we would be wise to look for clues in that letter.

The most obvious bit of help comes from 1 John 3:16, where we read, "We know love by this, that he laid down his life for us." In other words, the Christian belief that God is love is inseparable from, and best defined by, the events of Jesus' life and ministry, and especially His self-giving death on the Cross. If we say that God is love, we must also say that *the kind of love God is* has been revealed to us in Jesus' laying down of His life for our sakes. *We know love* (the Greek word here is *agape*) by this.

There is a basic Christian assumption at work here: Jesus' life and death demonstrate or reveal God's love to us. Jesus reveals God's essential character and being, giving us confidence to echo John's bold claim that "God is love."

But why Jesus? Why believe that His life in any way reveals God?

THE CRUCIAL ROLE OF THE WRITINGS OF JOHN

Christians of the first few centuries thought long and hard on these questions. The answer they arrived at depends a great deal on the writings of the New Testament, particularly the writings of John and Paul. Finally it comes down to the simple claim that "Jesus is the Son of God" (1 John 4:15). This *love that God is* "was revealed among us in this way: God sent his only Son into the world so that we might live through him. In this is love, not that we loved God but that God loved us and sent his Son to be the atoning sacrifice for our sins" (1 John 4:9-10).

This reminds us that the Christian doctrine of God points to a fundamentally unique portrait of the divine nature. God isn't "simply God" or God "all alone." *God has a Son*—and always has! "In the beginning was the Word, and the Word was with God, and the Word was God" (John 1:1).

John's Gospel opens famously with this mind-bender: the Word (a translation of the Greek term *logos*) was *with* God and thus is *not simply the same as* God. In the original Greek text, even the last phrase of that opening verse —usually translated as "the Word was God"—does not teach that this Word was simply identical with God. It is not as though "God" and "the Word" are nothing but interchangeable terms. Instead, the meaning of the Greek text is essentially that this Word shared fully in God's character and being. The *Revised English Bible,* for example, offers the translation "what God was, the Word was."

It is this Word that "became flesh and lived among us" (John 1:14). This is what we mean by the theological term "incarnation"—the Word that was with God and shared fully in God's being truly became human. The Word that is God actually entered into and authentically participated in our creaturely realm. This incarnate Word is the Son, Jesus Christ, "who is close to the Father's heart." It is Jesus "who has made God known" (John 1:18).

We know that God is love through Jesus' great love for His disciples. In His final conversation with the disciples, Jesus tells them (and us), "As the Father has loved me, so I have loved you" (John 15:9). In other words, Jesus shares fully with us the love that God the Father shares with Him. He instructs His disciples to "abide" (or "hang out," in popular lingo) "in my love" (v. 9). How do we abide in Jesus' love? He tells us: "If you keep my commandments, you will abide in my love, just as I have kept my Father's commandments and abide in his love" (v. 10).

At this point, people tend to speculate about which commandments, exactly, Jesus has in mind. Of course, one could answer, "*All* of them." But we often find ourselves gravitating toward the Ten Commandments as a good place to start. In any case, it is precisely at this point that we could fall into the old trap of thinking of holiness as rule-keeping.

It seems best to us to stay with the text of John 15 to answer this question: "Which commandments?" In the next breath Jesus actually spells out what "commandments" He has in mind. And strangely enough, His list of commandments is strikingly short. "This is my commandment, that you love one another as I have loved you" (15:12). Jesus' commandments have been reduced to a single commandment.

It would appear that Jesus is boiling down into a single thing what it means to be His follower: love one another. Of course, this doesn't mean love is easy. Remember that Jesus said earlier that He loves us just as the Father loves Him. That's amazing love! This seems to be something like a chain reaction: God the Father loves the Son, who in turn and in the same way loves His disciples, who in turn and in the same way are to love one another.

In John's Gospel, then, we find the possibility that we can so truly experience God's love through Jesus that we are actually enabled to love in a similar way. But how does that happen? Is it enough simply to say, "The Father loves the Son, and the Son passes that love on to you—now get busy and start loving in the same way"? We don't think so.

In this same conversation, Jesus talks about a "Helper" or "Comforter." The words represent two possible ways to translate the Greek word *paraclete* (literally, "one called to be alongside"). This helper is "the Holy Spirit," said Jesus, who will "be with you forever" and "will teach you everything, and remind you of all that I have said to you" (John 14:16, 26).

Jesus tells us that the Holy Spirit *makes real to us* this great love of the Father for the Son. When Jesus says that He and His Father "will love [the disciples], and . . . will come to them and make our home with them" (14:23), it seems appropriate to interpret this task of home-making to the Spirit. The Holy Spirit brings God—God understood as *the Father and the Son loving each other*—right down to our level, our experience, our lives, each moment. Christians throughout the history of the Church deduce the following: if the Holy Spirit really, truly brings this divine love —this love-of-the-Father-for-the-Son—to us, then this Holy Spirit *must somehow be God too.* This makes our description of God even more complex.

We find God powerfully portrayed in this way near the end of John's Gospel. We read that the resurrected Jesus said to His frightened disciples, "As the Father has sent me, so I send you." Then Jesus breathed on them with the words "Receive the Holy Spirit" (20:21-22).

The English word "spirit" is a translation of biblical

words that mean "wind" or "breath," so it is appropriate that Jesus *breathes* this Holy Spirit upon His disciples. This denotes the Spirit's close and intimate relation to Jesus and the Spirit's indwelling intimacy with Jesus' disciples. The Spirit is something like the life-breath and whisper of love from the Father to the Son, freely blown toward and into us who would be Jesus' followers. As this Spirit, God whispers to us moment-by-moment, every step of our adventure.

When Jesus prays in John 17 for His disciples, we see that this in-breathed Helper is thoroughly and deeply implied. Jesus' prayer is that His followers down through the ages "all . . . may be one, Father, just as you are in me and I am in you" (v. 21, NIV).

For the Father to be "in Jesus" and for Jesus to be "in the Father" requires that we think in profoundly relational ways. Just as in chapter one we explored the idea that our lives are deeply intertwined with one another, we see now that this is in fact the very nature of God: *the Father in the Son and the Son in the Father*. Here we do not encounter a pair of isolated egos or entirely separate subjects. Instead, we encounter two mutually indwelling identities of Father and Son. It would seem that these two share in the same Spirit!

But perhaps even more remarkable is Jesus' next request: *"May they also be in us"* (17:21, NIV, emphasis added). There is no doubt that we cannot fully understand what it means for us, Jesus' disciples, to "be in" the Father and the Son. But it does imply that somehow Jesus' prayer is that we shall actually be drawn into, and dwell within, this mutually indwelling relationship.

The Spirit is the Breath in whose life and presence we actually share in the mutual life and love of the Father and Son. Incredibly enough, John is pointing us toward the possibility that we may actually, and in this life, breathe deep of the life and love of God!

Perhaps it is not too much to suggest that because the Father and the Son "make room" for us in their common life of the Spirit, our common life together really makes a difference in God's own life and experience of the world. When we love one another as we are loved, we even contribute something that enriches God's own love! Surely when we so love, our lives are pleasing to God. In a real sense, being a blessing to others means also being a blessing to God.

process theol. ?

"The glory that you have given me I have given them," Jesus prays, "so that they may be one, as we are one. *I in them* and *you in me*, that they may become *completely one*" (vv. 22-23, emphasis added). Jesus is praying that we who are Jesus' disciples and followers, His Church, might actually live and embody divine love and unity through the inbreathed, empowering presence of the Spirit.

SHARING IN THE TRIUNE LOVE THAT IS GOD

Such themes as these, found especially though not exclusively in John's New Testament writings, provide the raw material for a great deal of exciting thinking about the Trinity. One of the truly important implications of the

Trinity is that this relationship among Father, Son, and Holy Spirit—a dynamic sharing of self-giving, other-receiving love—is God's essential nature. *It is who, and what, God is*, always and eternally. God *is* this richly complex relational matrix and ever shall be.

What has been revealed of God in the sending of the Son and the outpouring of the Spirit is God's own being-in-love. Other statements, claims, or ideas about God must be submitted to this criterion summarized in the Christian doctrine of God as an eternal, triune communion of love.

In this line of thinking, we find it compelling to interpret Christian holiness as our active participation in the love between God the Father and God the Son through the power and presence of God the Spirit. This love that God is—revealed to us through Jesus' openhearted laying-down of His life for us—ideally ought to be experienced. And we experience this because the Holy Spirit labors among us, especially within the loving fellowship of the Church.

We know what love is because God has revealed love in Jesus' self-outpoured ministry and crucifixion. The presence and power of the Holy Spirit continue the work of extending that love to us, making it *real*. "And by this we know that he abides in us, by the Spirit that he has given us" (1 John 3:24).

Just as God has given us this Spirit to abide within and among us, 1 John also gives us a criterion for detecting this Spirit. We are to "test the spirits to see whether they are from God." The test for recognizing the work of "the Spirit of God" is that "every spirit that confesses that Jesus Christ has come in the flesh is from God" (4:1-2). Remarkable!

John is telling us that the Spirit's role is always to direct us toward the truly incarnate Christ, toward the Word who became flesh and lived among us. The Spirit who comes from God is always leading us to Jesus—to this particular and historical human who "laid down his life for us" (1 John 3:16).

No wonder 1 John does not simply leave the matter at what we touched on earlier: that "We know love by this, that he laid down his life for us" (3:16). Important as that is, it is equally important to keep reading: "and we ought to lay down our lives for one another." John's Gospel teaches us to see that in Jesus' laying-down of His life for us, we are receiving a profound glimpse into the eternal nature of God—and that in the power of Jesus' out-breathed Spirit upon and within us, we can share in that love with one another in practical, everyday ways.

It is important to keep reading the 1 John passage further in order not to become too theoretical, too speculative, or even too "spiritual" about what it might mean to love. The biblical writer immediately provides a down-home illustration of what he means: "How does God's love abide in anyone who has the world's goods and sees a brother or sister in need and yet refuses to help?" (3:17). It will hopefully be clear just how nicely our working definition for love—acting to promote well-being in the lives of others—corresponds to this biblical passage.

The love and unity between the Father and the Son in

the presence of the Spirit is continually being shared with those who are receptive to this living flow. It is a shared life, a life of communion. And as such, it is communicated in practical ways as the sharing of *life* and the *goods of life* with one another.

THE WITNESS OF THE SPIRIT

Surely in John's writings this kind of mutually sharing and shared life, the life of loving "fellowship" (1 John 1:3), is the essence of holiness. It means "to walk just as [Jesus] walked" (2:6), which simply means to "love one another, just as he has commanded us" (3:23). Following a pattern of John Wesley, we might say that holiness is Christlikeness. Christlikeness entails self-giving, other-receiving love. Wesley described the entirely sanctified believer in his little classic *A Plain Account of Christian Perfection*:

> We mean one in whom is "the mind which was in Christ," and who so "walketh as Christ also walked"; . . . He "loveth the Lord his God with all his heart," and serveth him "with all his strength." He "loveth his neighbor," every man, "as himself"; yea, "as Christ loveth us"; . . . Indeed, his soul is all love.

It is important to add that Wesley insisted that such a love for God and neighbor is not something we generate out of our own willpower or energies. He insisted that we can love in this way only if we have first experienced this love of the triune God for ourselves.

This experience of divine love, in turn, is precisely what the Holy Spirit inspires within us. Wesley was prone to quote Paul's good news that "God's love has been poured into our hearts through the Holy Spirit that has been given to us" (Rom. 5:5). Further, he asked a good follow-up question: if God's love really is poured into our hearts through the Holy Spirit, should we not actually be able to experience this? Should we not in some way be able to *feel* God's love?

Wesley insisted that feeling God's love ought to characterize the Christian's life with God in both its early stages and later, more mature ones. His point in insisting on this was to place the priority on God's love for and within us rather than on our attempts to love God and others.

Drawing on passages in Paul's letters, Wesley called this experience "the witness of the Spirit." "We must love God before we can be holy at all, this being the root of all holiness," he suggests. For "we cannot love God, till we know He loves us: 'We love him, because He first loved us'; and we cannot know His love to us, till His Spirit witnesses it to our spirit."

In Gal. 4:6, Paul writes of this witness in dramatically Trinitarian terms. "Because you are [God's] children," writes Paul, "God has sent the Spirit of his Son into our hearts, crying, 'Abba! Father!'" Interestingly, Paul uses the same verb (*exapostello* = "sent forth") just two verses earlier to refer to the sending of the Son in "the fullness of time" (4:4). So we could say that Paul writes that God first *sent forth* the Son into history and under the conditions of history ("born of a woman, born under the law"), and God *sent forth* the Spirit of the Son into our hearts.

The Father sent the Son into our history, into the human stream, as a Jew of a particular place and time. This is the Incarnation of the divine Son. Yet God has also sent the Spirit, whom Paul identifies as "the Spirit of God's Son," into human hearts.

Sending the Son indicates an exterior, objective, historical event in the history of our planet. Sending the Spirit of the Son indicates an interior, subjective, experience of God's great love—a love revealed to us in and through the life and ministry of the Son. The Spirit is the outpouring, the outbreathing, of God toward creation. Because the Spirit flows to us in and through the life, words, and works of Jesus, that Spirit comes to us as shaped and informed by Jesus. Hence, the Spirit of God is the Spirit of God's Son.

Texts such as this help us get a sense for the dynamism of the triune God. God is *One who sends forth*. God sends forth the Son in the power of the Spirit. And God sends forth the Spirit in the name and identity of the Son, that is, *through* the Son, into our hearts. *In the gift of the Spirit we receive the Spirit of the God who gives the Son to the world.* Thus we receive the dynamic outflow of the very life and love of the triune God. We receive the very life of God, which is the very love of God, when we receive God's gift of the Spirit.

As far as John Wesley was concerned, we are dealing here with the practical gist of the Christian doctrine of the Trinity. In his only sermon devoted to this doctrine, Wesley insists that the doctrine of "the Three-One God . . . lies at the root of all vital religion." It "is interwoven with all true Christian faith."

There was for Wesley a very simple reason for this. The

bottom line is the witness of the Spirit. He writes very near the sermon's end, "But I know not how any one can be a Christian believer . . . 'til God the Holy Ghost witnesses that God the Father has accepted him through the merits of God the Son: And, having this witness, he honours the Son, and the blessed Spirit, 'even as he honours the Father.'"

We see the connections between holiness as a life of love, the witness of the Spirit, and the doctrine of the Trinity. We are called to love God with all our energies and to love our neighbor as ourselves. But we can love like this only when we know, deeply, that we are loved. And we can know this only as God's Spirit imparts to our hearts, in the deepest recesses of our beings, that we are unconditionally loved by God.

The Spirit who witnesses in our hearts is the Spirit of the Son who cries out to the Father, "Abba!" To receive into our hearts the Spirit whom God sends forth is, at the very same time, to be drawn into this very life of the triune God. For the triune life is true life—the life of lovingly and deeply shared communion.

The question we will save for the next chapter is this: What is it like to share in this Trinitarian life of God? Can we actually experience this life, as Wesley insisted? For lack of a better way to put it, What does the witness of the Spirit feel like?

QUESTIONS TO STIMULATE DISCUSSION

1. How does reflection on the Trinity help us understand better the sentence "God is love"?

2. The writer of John's Gospel says that the Word was *with God*—and thus He is *not identical to* God. What might this mean for understanding Jesus as revealing God?

3. It is sometimes said that we know what God looks like when we see Jesus. How does this chapter affect this saying?

4. Jesus compresses all of the commandments to a single commandment: "Love one another as I have loved you" (John 15:12). How might we imitate the love of Jesus?

5. How might conceiving of holiness as love help us understand Jesus' prayer that His disciples be *in* God?

6. How might it be important to believe, and "feel," that God loves us?

7. How might God as Spirit inspire love in us?

FOR DEEPER STUDY

Baker, Anthony D. "Violence and the Trinity: A Wesleyan Reading of Milbank's Augustinianism." *Wesleyan Theological Journal* 36:1 (spring 2001).

Blevins, Dean G. "The Trinity and the Means of Grace: A Sacramental Interrelationship." *Wesleyan Theological Journal* 36:1 (spring 2001).

Braaten, Laurie J. "The Voice of Wisdom: A Creation Context for Proto-Trinitarian Thought." *Wesleyan Theological Journal* 36:1 (spring 2001).

Bryant, Barry E. "Trinity and Hymnody: The Doctrine of the Trinity in the Hymns of Charles Wesley." *Wesleyan Theological Journal* 25:2 (fall 1990).

Collins, Kenneth J. "A Reconfiguration of Power: The Basic Trajectory of John Wesley's Practical Theology." *Wesleyan Theological Journal* 33:1 (spring 1998).

Coppedge, Allan. *Portraits of God: A Biblical Theology of Holiness.* Downers Grove, Ill.: InterVarsity Press, 2001.

Dunning, H. Ray. *Reflecting the Divine Image: Christian Ethics in Wesleyan Perspective.* Downers Grove, Ill.: InterVarsity Press, 1998.

Greathouse, William M. *From the Apostles to Wesley. Christian Perfection in Historical Perspective.* Kansas City: Beacon Hill Press of Kansas City, 1979.

Grider, Kenneth J. *A Wesleyan-Holiness Theology.* Kansas City: Beacon Hill Press of Kansas City, 1994.

Kendall, David. *Is Holiness Really Possible?* Kansas City: Beacon Hill Press of Kansas City, 2000.

LaCugna, Catherine Mowry. *God for Us: The Trinity and Christian Life.* San Francisco: HarperSanFrancisco, 1991.

Lancaster, Sarah. "Women, Wesley, and Original Sin." *Quarterly Review* 23:4 (winter 2003).

Leupp, Roderick. "Flames of Holy Love: John Wesley's Trinitarian Faith." *Herald of Holiness*, June 1998.

———. *Knowing the Name of God: A Trinitarian Tapestry of Grace, Faith, and Community.* Downers Grove, Ill.: InterVarsity Press, 1996.

Lodahl, Michael. *"Una Natura Divina, Tres Nescio Quid:* What Sorts of *Personae* Are Divine *Personae?" Wesleyan Theological Journal* 36:1 (spring 2001).

McCormick, K. Steve. "The Heresies of Love." *Wesleyan Theological Journal* 37:1 (spring 2002).

Meadows, Philip R., ed. *Windows on Wesley: Wesleyan Theology for To-day's World.* Oxford, England: Applied Theology Press, 1997.

Powell, Samuel M. "Divine Trinity." In *Philosophy of Religion: Introductory Essays.* Edited by Thomas Jay Oord. Kansas City: Beacon Hill Press of Kansas City, 2003.

———. "The Doctrine of the Trinity in 19th-Century American Wesleyan Theology." *Wesleyan Theological Journal* 18:2 (fall 1983).

———. *Participating in God: Trinity and Creation.* Philadelphia: Fortress Press, 2003.

Runyon, Theodore. "Holiness as the Renewal of the Image of God in the Individual and Society." In *Embodied Holiness: Toward a Corporate Theology of Spiritual Growth.* Edited by Samuel M. Powell and Michael E. Lodahl. Downers Grove, Ill: InterVarsity Press, 1999.

Severson, Eric. "Ethical Dialogue: Trinitarian Externality as a Pattern for Evangelism and Missions." *Wesleyan Theological Journal* 38:1 (spring 2003).

Torrance, James B. *Worship, Community and the Triune God of Grace.* Downers Grove, Ill.: InterVarsity Press, 1996.

Wynkoop, Mildred Bangs. "A Hermeneutical Approach to John Wesley." *Wesleyan Theological Journal* 6:1 (spring 1971).

5
Loving Practice Makes Perfect Love

As we have seen, John Wesley, along with a host of other Christian leaders and thinkers through the centuries, often insisted that true holiness consists of love for God and neighbor. He also proclaimed that this holiness is a real possibility in this life by the redemptive power of God. This power is none other than God's matchless love. Divine love outpoured through Jesus Christ in the power of the Spirit can so fill our hearts that in this very moment—and in the next—we can truly love God, our neighbors, and God's creation, including ourselves.

Of course, there is always room for growth in love. The journey we are on moves us dynamically toward an increasing likeness of the character of Jesus Christ. Wesley believed deeply in the real possibility of the transforming grace of God to *heal* human hearts and lives, "renewing us in love," as he often put it. Christian perfection is, in its essence, *perfection in love*.

Additionally, Wesley insisted that this love for God is not possible unless and until we *know* that God loves us. And we cannot know that God loves us, Wesley continued, unless and until the Spirit "bears witness" and assures us of this love.

All of this leads to questions that call out for practical and concrete replies: Is there truly available an experience of God that can touch our hearts and lives so deeply that we may become renewed and empowered to love? And if there is, how does this occur? As we asked at the conclusion of chapter four, what does this love "feel like"?

Wesley insisted that true Christians can, and normally should expect to, undergo an experience of the Holy Spirit's testimony to assure them of God's redeeming love. He preached that the Spirit's witness is one of the peculiar privileges of the children of God. And his theological heirs have a particular stake in the doctrine, because it is one grand part of the testimony that God has given them to bear to all creation.

Such an experience continues to be expected, at least officially, in denominations that bear the Wesleyan stamp. For example, the Church of the Nazarene's articles of faith on regeneration and entire sanctification both include the phrase "and to this work and state of grace the Holy Spirit bears witness."

Wesley was convinced that if God works graciously in our hearts and lives, we should be aware of God's working to some extent and in some way. Nevertheless, he did not think that everyone's supposed experiences of God were authentic. After all, people can imagine that God is telling them to do some pretty wild things! All apparently religious experiences were to be judged by Scripture and reason. Even more basically, the tests of Scripture and reason were to be exercised collectively in and by the Church, which is the community of Christian faith and practice.

In his book *The New Creation: John Wesley's Theology Today*, Theodore Runyon discusses how Wesley dealt with those who criticized his emphasis upon the witness of the Spirit. "To the skeptic who question[ed] the possibility of any such contact with transcendent reality," Runyon writes, "Wesley did not reply with rational arguments. . . . Instead, Wesley invited the skeptic to attend the meeting of a local society, to become a member of a class, which proved to be the best apologetic method, because it invited a skeptic to be open to a new community of experience."

This concept of a "new community of experience" is important, for it picks up out of Wesley's writings a *social* model for experiencing God. When summarizing Wesley's notion of "social grace," Runyon writes,

If Christian faith is brought into existence by receiving divine mercy and love, it cannot be contained within the isolated individual. What is received demands further expression; that is its nature. If what comes to us is God's loving though not uncritical affirmation, this affirmation cannot be hoarded but must be shared. The love *to* us from the world's Savior flows *through* us to all the world's creatures, especially to those in need and distress. "Whatever grace you have received of God may through you be communicated to others" ([Nashville: Abingdon Press, 1998], 163).

To explore this social model of experiencing the Spirit that Runyon suggests, we will need to do some disciplined thinking. Generally speaking, the doctrine of the Spirit's testimony tends to be understood today in an individualistic rather than relational way. Wesley gradually came to understand our experience of God as occurring often through the social networks provided by the Church. His ministry provided a powerful social context for what he proclaimed in his sermons. The listeners of these sermons were continually being encouraged to be involved in small-group meetings, in weekly worship and participation in the Lord's Supper, and in other forms of what Wesley liked to call "social graces."

How Can We Know That God Loves Us?

In his sermons titled "The Witness of the Spirit," Wesley appeals to 1 John as support for insisting that our love for God is a *response* to God's love. This love is actually *felt* in the heart by the testimony of the Spirit. The biblical text, as Wesley quotes it, is "We love him, because he first loved us" (4:19, KJV). At the point of this verse and within its context, we need to return to Wesley's doctrine of the assurance of God's love.

Many of us grew up singing a chorus that went, "O how I love Jesus, Because He first loved me." Those lyrics clearly were inspired by 1 John 4:19. However, most of the ear-

liest Greek manuscripts actually read, "We love because
He first loved us." In other words, God is not explicitly
mentioned as the object of our love. Not that God is to be
excluded. But the immediate context of the statement,
not to mention the larger setting of 1 John, suggests that
we love *one another*—or at least *ought* to love one another—because God loves us. The very next verse insists that
"those who do not love a brother or sister whom they have
seen, cannot love God whom they have not seen" (4:20).
Jesus' disciples are to love each other.

What difference, you might ask, does it make to read
1 John 4:19 as referring primarily to our love for one another? So what if John's message is not so much that we love
God because God first loved us, but that we love *one another* in the Christian community because God first loved
us? We are suggesting that this verse provides a foundation
for Wesley's thinking on the nature of God's love and how
that love can be a transforming, healing, and *perceptible*
power—a power we can actually experience.

We have seen repeatedly that Wesley insisted that
grace is perceptible by virtue of the power and presence of
the Holy Spirit in human life. But with the help of 1 John,
we may supplement Wesley's notion by thinking about the
transforming power of the Spirit in a different way. This
way takes with utmost seriousness the importance of local church congregations.

Notice some repeated themes in John's epistle:

- 1 John 1:1—"What was *from the beginning* . . . was
  the word of life" (emphasis added), the divine Word

that has been heard, seen, and touched (the Word become flesh of John 1:14). Because this Word was a human being, it was an eminently *perceptible* Word from God to us.

- 1 John 2:7—"An old commandment . . . *from the beginning* . . . is the word that you have heard" (emphasis added). The use again of the phrase "from the beginning" makes it easy to associate the Word that has been heard, seen, and touched (in the opening passage of the letter) with this "word that you have heard" in chapter two.

- 1 John 3:11—"For this is the message you have heard *from the beginning,* that we *should love one another*" (emphasis added). Now we learn the nature of the command or Word that we have heard "from the beginning." Given the message of John's Gospel and this first letter of John, it should come as no surprise that this message, this communication from God, is most essentially that we who are disciples of Jesus are to love one another.

God's grace is *perceptible* (or able to be felt) first of all in the Word of life that dwelt among us: Jesus Christ. Further, this word that was *from the beginning*—meaning perhaps from the eternal heart of God—is a word or message of *love for one another*. Because this same letter tells us that "God is love," it only makes sense that God's Word to all who believe that God is love is that we should share in the divine love with one another.

Although the Word of life is no longer directly perceptible for human beings (that is, Jesus no longer walks and talks among us as a physical human presence), the reality and effects of that Word ought even today to be perceptible in the gatherings of Jesus' disciples for worship and edification (churches). The love of God in Christ ought to be a love that is visible, touchable, experiential, in the fellowship of any and every Christian congregation. This idea, in fact, is borne out in the following text from the same letter:

- 1 John 3:16—"*We know love by this*, that he laid down his life for us—and *we ought* to lay down our lives for one another" (emphasis added). If God's love for us is visible *in principle* in the historical act of Jesus' self-offering for us on the Cross, it also should be visible *in reality* in our own time. It is visible in any Christian congregation that shares in the self-giving, other-receiving love of God (see 3:17).

God's love, then, is perceptible to our senses: visible, touchable—or at least ought to be—in church communions where the *word which you have heard from the beginning* is heard and acted upon faithfully, boldly, and bodily. Relational holiness recognizes just how crucial is the love we give and receive from one another in our local Christian congregations. While not the only way we may truly experience God's love for us, it is a profoundly important way.

- 1 John 4:11-12 sums this up well: "Beloved, since God loved us so much, *we also ought to love one another*. No one has ever seen God; if we love one another, God lives in us, and *his love is perfected in us*" (emphasis added).

To summarize the argument of this chapter so far: in John's epistle we read of *the Word of life* that is also a *commandment* that we have *heard from the beginning*. From the very heart of God, a Word has issued forth from eternity to us that we *should love one another*. Because God is love, it figures that God's deepest goal and intention for creation should be that *God's love is received and shared*. In Jesus' sacrificial laying down of His life for us, that love is revealed and given content: *we know love by this, and we ought so to love one another*. In fact, if we love one another, then God's love is *perfected*—God's love finds its fulfillment, God's love accomplishes its purpose—in or among us (4:12).

With the apostle John's help, we have relocated the assurance of divine love in the *perceptible grace* of the Christian community. And this love can be heard, seen, and touched. Such love was *from the beginning*, for it proceeds from the very heart of God. This love became perceptible in the *Word of life* (Jesus Christ), particularly in His death on our behalf. And this love is shared in perceptible and palpable ways in local church congregations.

The Word of life is to be realized and "made true" not only historically in the person of Jesus but also in the present through our very life together as Christ's community of love. "If we love one another, God [the invisible and imperceptible One] lives in us" (4:12). When this happens, we can and do actually feel God's love. Now that's assurance!

While this social model perhaps goes a little beyond Wesley's own thinking about the witness of the Spirit, he was aware of this interpersonal and social dimension of God's labors in our lives. He spoke not simply of "social holiness" but of "social grace"—God's loving, active, healing presence mediated and flowing through others to us, and through us to others. He writes in his classic *A Plain Account of Christian Perfection,*

> Although all the graces of God depend on his mere bounty, yet is he pleased generally to attach them to the prayers, the instructions, and the holiness of *those with whom we are.* By strong, though invisible attractions, he draws some souls through their *intercourse with others* (emphasis added).

We do not mean to suggest that God's assuring and *reas-*suring presence is limited to flowing *only* through our human relationships. Wesley certainly would not have thought so. In his sermon, "The Means of Grace," he writes,

> [It] behooves us . . . always to retain a lively sense that God is above all means. Have a care, therefore, of limiting the Almighty. He doeth whatsoever and whensoever it pleaseth him. He can convey his grace, either in or out of any of the means which he hath appointed. Perhaps he will. . . . Look then every moment for his appearing!

In other words, we are on solid Wesleyan ground to assume that God whispers directly to us—and we at least occasionally sense that still, small Voice.

It is significant that Wesley placed such a decisive emphasis upon the means of divine grace—including and especially the network of relations bonded by Christ's love in Christian community. Yet he did not believe that all experience of divine grace occurs in this way. Perhaps we may employ one of Wesley's favorite phrases: that God's *ordinary means* of drawing us, wooing us, and assuring us of divine love is "by strong, though invisible attractions . . . [of] intercourse with others." That, however, does not and cannot exclude the possibility of *extraordinary* occasions and experiences of divine presence and love given to us through the direct workings of the Spirit within us.

For the most part, however, our problem has not been ignoring the concept of the work of the Holy Spirit within us. It has been ignoring the critical importance of the local church as the social matrix of the Spirit's labors.

This point is not difficult to illustrate. Many of us who were raised in Holiness churches heard plenty of sermons on the text "Don't you know that you yourselves are God's temple and that God's Spirit lives in you? If anyone destroys God's temple, God will destroy him; for God's temple is sacred, and you are that temple" (1 Cor. 3:16-17, NIV).

The typical Holiness sermon from this text assumed an individualistic premise: each of our bodies is God's temple, and we should not destroy that temple by smoking, drinking, or otherwise abusing this temple. (Conveniently, little was ever said in such sermons about overeating at church potluck dinners or getting hooked on caffeine!) However, to understand Paul's words in this individualistic and legalistic way is to ignore both the context and the Greek grammar he employs.

First, the context. Paul has just been chastising the

Corinthian believers for their divisive cliques and arguments of superiority over one another (3:1-4). The entire
chapter is devoted to undermining such divisiveness in
the church. Paul isn't saying a word here about how we
treat our own bodies. (He will do that a little later, in 1 Cor.
6.) So when Paul warns, "If anyone destroys God's temple,
God will destroy him," the context alone is enough to suggest that this temple is not an individual body but the
church itself.

Next, the grammar. Paul's point is clarified by understanding that the use of the second-person pronoun
"you" is repeatedly in the plural. If Paul had been a South-
ern preacher, he would have been using "you all." The
New International Version of the Bible helps us see this by
using "you yourselves" in one instance.

Let us spell out the Greek clearly here: "Don't you all
know that you all are *God's temple* (i.e., not a collection of
individual temples) and that God's Spirit lives in you all? If
anyone destroys God's temple, God will destroy him; for
God's temple is sacred, and you all are that temple."

The destruction of God's temple against which Paul
warns is the divisive attitudes and practices that were
threatening to disintegrate the Corinthian church. Paul
insists that the gift of the Spirit is shared among all Christian believers, not merely an individual possession.

Paul makes the same point in his letter to the Ephesians: "In [Christ] the whole building is joined together
and rises to become a holy temple in the Lord. And in him
you [*you all*] too *are being built together* to become a

dwelling in which God lives by his Spirit" (Eph. 2:21-22, NIV, emphasis added). Given that the Spirit is shared among us in such a way that we together make up God's place of dwelling, it behooves us to treat one another with utmost care, love, and respect. We see that the Holiness message of 1 Cor. 3 is not really about keeping our individual bodies clean and pure but about striving to keep our local congregations unified in the love of God.

Of course, this is not particularly easy to do. The letter to the Ephesians suggests hard labor when it encourages us to "make every effort to keep the unity of the Spirit through the bond of peace" (4.3, NIV). To "make every effort" suggests some work on our part.

Wesley put it even more strongly in advice he offers Christians who believe they have been entirely sanctified: "God is the first object of our love: its next office is, to bear the defects of others. And we should begin the practice of this amidst our own household." We should never forget, on the other hand, that those "others" have the unenviable job of bearing with *our* "defects"!

The local church congregation is our testing ground for love. It is the context of social relations in which Jesus' disciples are called upon to love and care for one another. The church is where we learn about God's love and what that love requires of us. The church is a place where we practice this kind of loving week in and week out—and practice makes perfect. As we live together in Christian community, we learn how to respond appropriately time and again to what is required to keep such community alive and thriving.

PRACTICES OF A LOVE COMMUNITY

Paul teaches us that one of the most important church practices for shaping our lives in Christian love is the Lord's Supper. The church divisions were so sharp in the Corinthian congregation that Paul flatly wrote that "when you come together, it is not the Lord's Supper you eat" (1 Cor. 11:20, NIV). And why not? Because "as you eat, each of you goes ahead without waiting for anybody else. One remains hungry, another gets drunk" (v. 21, NIV).

It appears that one of the divisive factors in this church was an economic one. Paul goes on to write that some of the Corinthian Christians "despise the church of God, and humiliate those who have nothing" (v. 22, NIV). The believers in the congregation who "remain hungry" are presumably "those who have nothing."

Paul asks this fractured body of Christ to remember what he had taught them about Jesus' final supper with His disciples. Jesus took bread, offered thanks to God, broke the bread, and shared it freely with His disciples. There was no smallness of spirit in Jesus' act; it was His body and blood freely given.

In the spirit of Jesus, Paul encouraged the Corinthians to share in the Supper and thus in Jesus' love. "For anyone who eats and drinks without recognizing the body of the Lord"—that is, without recognizing all the members of Christ's body, rich or poor, gathered to share together in the Supper—"eats and drinks judgment on himself" (11:29, NIV).

The bottom line for Paul is, "When you come together to eat, wait for each other" (v. 33, NIV). In demonstrating love and respect by waiting for each other and sharing in the supper of Jesus, God could make this fragmented collection of ragtag believers into the Body of Christ (1 Cor. 10:16-17).

This Lord's Supper passage illustrates how a variety of church practices—reading the Scriptures in unison, hearing them together being read and proclaimed, praying together, confessing our sins and faults to one another, participating together in the sacraments of baptism and the Lord's Supper—help us to love as God loves. And these practices help us have a better idea about what such love might require in any given context.

All of this should spur us to appreciate the crucial role of a compassionate and faithful Christian community for holy living. It supports well the understanding of relational holiness that we are promoting. If God indwells each Christian congregation to make it "a holy temple in the Lord," the Spirit lives in and among us, flowing through us to others and through others to us. God's gentle calling often woos us through the love of others. God's love can touch others through us, and touch us through others. No wonder the beloved apostle wrote that while no one has ever seen God, if we love one another, God lives in us, and God's love is perfected in us.

How much more important is it, then, for the person who has lost an inner assurance of God's love and grace to stay in the church? Such a person is the one who most desperately needs the reassurance of divine love given through the interpersonal bonds of Jesus' disciples.

yes! Unfortunately, there have been times when the doctrine of the witness of the Spirit was described as kind of a divine *zap*, a one-time, single-shot experience of "assurance" that was supposed to be adequate for the rest of one's life. We have suggested in this chapter, however, that the doctrine should be understood more dynamically and more relationally within the context of the local church congregation and its practices. It is found in what Wesley described as "the prayers, the instructions, and the holiness of those with whom we are." We affirm the central importance of the church as providing the interpersonal context in which the love of God can really, truly be *felt* in a bodily way—in the incarnational community that is the Body of Christ.

QUESTIONS TO STIMULATE DISCUSSION

1. Why do you think it is important to understand holiness in social rather than solely individualistic terms?

2. What do you think it means to *know* that God loves you? How might this knowledge influence the way you live life?

3. How can the Christian community become a way in which God's love is felt?

4. Of what importance are the Lord's Supper and baptism as expressions of love?

5. What are other community expressions of love?

6. In what ways have you felt assured of God's love, and how might you act to assure others?

7. How ought the Church to express God's love in what it says, does, and promotes?

FOR DEEPER STUDY

Blevins, Dean G. "Holy Church, Holy People." *Wesleyan Theological Journal* 39:2 (fall 2004).

―――. "The Means of Grace and the Trinity: A Sacramental Interrelationship." *Wesleyan Theological Journal* 36:1 (spring 2001).

―――. "Practicing the New Creation: Wesley's Eschatological Community Formed by the Means of Grace." *Asbury Theological Journal* 57:2 & 58:1 (fall 2002 and spring 2003).

―――. "We Are the Church: The Liturgical Construction of the Self." *Doxology: A Journal of Worship* 18 (2001).

Clapper, Gregory S. "Wesley's Main Doctrines: Spiritual Formation and Teaching in the Wesleyan Tradition." *Wesleyan Theological Journal* 39:2 (fall 2004).

Collins, Kenneth J. "John Wesley and the Means of Grace." *Drew Gateway* 56:3 (1986).

―――. "The Soteriological Orientation of John Wesley's Ministry to the Poor." *Asbury Theological Journal* 50:1 (1995).

Cubie, David L. "A Wesleyan Perspective on Christian Unity." *Wesleyan Theological Journal* 33:2 (fall 1998).

Dunning, H. Ray. "Christian Perfection: Toward a New Paradigm." *Wesleyan Theological Journal* 33:1 (spring 1998).

Gates, Jamie. "The Strength of Diversity." In *Generation Xers Talk About the Church of the Nazarene*. Edited by Thomas Jay Oord. Kansas City: Beacon Hill Press of Kansas City, 1999.

Harrison, Douglas Joel, and Cynthia Transmeier. "Toothpaste Jesus." In *Generation Xers Talk About the Church of the Nazarene*. Edited by Thomas Jay Oord. Kansas City: Beacon Hill Press of Kansas City, 1999.

Holiness 101: Exploring This Transforming Journey. Kansas City: Beacon Hill Press of Kansas City, 2003.

LeClerc, Diane. *Singleness of Heart: Gender, Sin, and Holiness in Historical Perspective*. Lanham, Md.: Scarecrow Press, 2001.

Maddox, Randy L. "'Visit the Poor': John Wesley, the Poor, and the Sanctification of Believers." In *The Wesleys and the Poor: The Legacy and Development of Methodist Attitudes to Poverty, 1729-1999.* Edited by Richard Heitzenrater. Nashville: Kingswood Press, 2002.

Meadows, Philip R. "Embodying Conversion." In *Conversion in the Wesleyan Tradition.* Edited by Kenneth J. Collins. Nashville: Abingdon Press, 2001.

Powell, Samuel. "A Contribution to a Wesleyan Understanding of Holiness and Community." In *Embodied Holiness: Toward a Corporate Theology of Spiritual Growth.* Edited by Samuel M. Powell and Michael E. Lodahl. Downers Grove, Ill.: InterVarsity Press, 1999.

Reed, Millard. "What Does God Require? (Ps. 24:3-4)." In *Biblical Resources for Holiness Preaching: From Text to Sermon.* Vol. 1, edited by H. Ray Dunning and Neil B. Wiseman. Kansas City: Beacon Hill Press of Kansas City, 1993.

Reed, Rodney Layne. *Holy with Integrity: The Unity of Personal and Social Ethics in the Holiness Movement, 1880-1910.* Salem, Ohio: Schmul Publishing Co., 2003.

Rowell, Jeren. "A Holy Church." In *Holiness 101: Exploring This Transforming Journey.* Kansas City: Beacon Hill Press of Kansas City, 2003.

Runyon, Theodore. *The New Creation: John Wesley's Theology Today.* Nashville: Abingdon Press, 1998.

Salter, Darius. *American Evangelism: Its Theology and Practice.* Grand Rapids: Baker Book House, 1996.

Schwanz, Judith A. "Honest to the Core." In *The Hunger of Your Heart: Finding Fulfillment Through a Closer Walk with God.* Edited by Wesley Tracy. Kansas City: Beacon Hill Press of Kansas City, 1998.

Severson, Eric R. "Absence Transformed: The Eucharistic Site of Christian Theology." *Wesleyan Theological Journal.* 39:2 (fall 2004).

Snyder, Howard A. *Liberating the Church: The Ecology of Church and Kingdom.* Downers Grove, Ill.: InterVarsity Press, 1983.

Spaulding, Henry W. "Practicing Holiness." *Wesleyan Theological Journal.* 40:1 (spring 2005).

Staples, Rob. *Outward Sign and Inward Grace: The Place of Sacraments in Wesleyan Spirituality.* Kansas City: Beacon Hill Press of Kansas City, 1991.

Stone, Bryan P. *Compassionate Ministry: Theological Foundations.*
    Maryknoll, N.Y.: Orbis Books, 1996.
Thompson, Richard P. "Community in Conversation: Multiple Read-
    ings of Scripture and a Wesleyan Understanding of the Church."
    Wesleyan Theological Journal 35:1 (spring 2000).
———. "'Where the Spirit of the Lord Is': God and the Church in the
    Book of Acts." *Wesleyan Theological Journal* 36:1 (spring 2001).
Weigelt, Morris. "Holiness and Integrity (2 Tim. 2:20-21)." In *Biblical
    Resources for Holiness Preaching: From Text to Sermon.* Vol. 2, edit-
    ed by H. Ray Dunning. Kansas City: Beacon Hill Press of Kansas
    City, 1993.

6
Dancers, Not Dinosaurs

We have discovered that love is the heart of holiness and that those who identify with the Holiness tradition ought to consider love as the core of their distincitve doctrine. The label "relational holiness" reminds us that love involves interactive relations with God and others. To act and be holy is to respond to God and others by living an adventure of love.

CONTRIBUTORY HOLINESS NOTIONS AS EXPRESSIONS OF LOVE

We must make good on a promise found in chapter two. We discovered there that biblical writers use the words "holy," "holiness," and "sanctification" to convey various meanings. While most of these meanings are important, all but one are contributory rather than core notions of holiness.

We promised to show how the contributory notions of holiness add to a richer understanding of holiness as love. To use the metaphor we offered earlier, we now need to identify how the water, air, fire, and dirt notions of holiness express the atom of holiness: love.

Rules and Regulations

The apostle Paul tells us that love fulfills the intent of moral codes and rules found in the Bible. "The commandments, 'You shall not commit adultery; You shall not murder; You shall not steal; You shall not covet'; and any other commandment," writes Paul, "are summed up in this word, 'Love your neighbor as yourself.'" He adds, "Love does no wrong to a neighbor; therefore, love is the fulfilling of the law" (Rom. 13:9-10). In short, to love is to act rightly, and to act rightly is to love. Acting rightly—righteousness—is acting to promote well-being.

Because love fulfills the law, it subverts the legalism that inevitably arises when we equate holiness with following rules and regulations. After all, love is a law unto itself. A life of love provides the meaning and satisfaction that cannot be gained when we are ultimately concerned with observing a set of rules.

Closely related to following rules is the biblical command to obey God. The command to obey rubs the wrong way many who hear it. Obedience smacks of slavery and blind conformity. But when our loving God, who seeks to promote well-being, calls upon us to obey, our response ought to be different. Obedience to a loving God is not blind slavery, for we freely choose to respond to the One who has flourishing and abundant life in mind. In this response, obedience is the way of love.

Much of the time, rules and moral codes help us live life well. If we were to try to live without any rules, our lives would be chaotic and destructive. It is true that rules cannot replace love. And they must sometimes be broken in the name of love. But when we use rules as guides for living well, they become tools to decide what love might require. And the habits that emerge from love-based rules form our character in ways that reflect blessedness.

Purity

Love as the core of holiness helps us make sense of holiness as purity too. When we love, we act in a morally pure fashion. The life of love is the way of clean living, a life free from the filth of sin.

When we regard purity as a consequence of love, we skirt the negative side effects generated when purity is deemed the core notion of holiness. Unlike those who seek purity for its own sake, those who love do not seek isolation and detachment. Those who love do not retreat into their shells in an effort to remain pure but instead engage their world. Despite the difficulties and inconveniences that embracing others sometimes brings, those who love are not morally desecrated or dirtied. Love does not pollute. Love excludes sin.

Charissa's story illustrates this love-inspired shift from reactive to proactive behavior. Charissa worked tirelessly to keep the rules of Christianity and to remain pure. She was on constant guard to avoid appearing as though she might do evil. She feared that even a slight misstep would ruin her quality of life and reputation, both today and in the hereafter.

Charissa suffered from spiritual paranoia. Existing in such a state is worrisome, grueling, and joyless. She strained under the heavy load of legalistic living. Being religious had become exhausting, and she was beginning to feel as if she needed a break from religion.

When reading her Bible one day, Charissa came across these words of Jesus: "Come to me, all you that are weary and are carrying heavy burdens, and I will give you rest. Take my yoke upon you, and learn from me; for I am gentle and humble in heart, and you will find rest for your souls. For my yoke is easy, and my burden is light" (Matt. 11:28-30).

The idea that living the Christian life could be easy and light was foreign to Charissa. After reading these liberating verses, she confessed her need for rest and direction. In response to God's empowering presence, she changed her aim in life. This change did not mean that Charissa no longer faced hardship. It did mean, however, that she was liberated from thinking that Christianity was concerned primarily with fanatical legalism and paralyzing purity.

Instead of concentrating upon avoiding evil, Charissa concentrated her energy upon doing good. Instead of being paranoid, she determined to live a life of love. What a difference this reorientation made!

Total Commitment

Charissa's story provides a natural segue to the third contributory notion of holiness to reconsider in the light of love: total commitment. While not itself the core of holiness, total commitment to a loving God and to God's call of love is the core. To be more specific, a lifestyle of love requires absolute devotion to what the Ultimate Lover and love requests. We express holiness best when we love God, others, and (in appropriate ways) ourselves.

We earlier criticized the idea that total commitment could be the core notion of holiness, because by itself, total commitment is vague. One could be committed to just about anything or any type of God. This vagueness is overcome when we understand holiness as complete devotion to the One who has shown us such great love and who calls us to the love that promotes flourishing.

Kierkegaard's quotation in chapter three asked for what we might live and die. To live and die for any cause, idea, or person is to show one's total commitment and unrelenting devotion. Love as expressed by God in each moment, as expressed in the life of Jesus Christ by the power of the Holy Spirit and as seen in responses by those around us (especially within the Christian community), is worth living and dying for. Love is the prize that makes running life's race worthwhile.

We know what love is through the revelation of God in Jesus Christ. We comprehend love by reflecting upon and sharing in the life of the triune God. If our holy God's nature and activity are love, it makes sense to say that we are holy when we love. To put it succinctly, we are holy when we love wholly.

Christlikeness

Reflecting upon the triune God also helps us understand Christlikeness. The exemplar approach to holiness is helpful when we regard Jesus as our model. It is helpful, that is, so long as we remember that what makes Jesus a worthy example is His love. This means that the general answer to the popular question "What would Jesus do?" is always "Jesus would love."

Unfortunately, one can interpret wrongly what it means to be Christlike. Examples of Christlikeness gone astray arise annually in present-day Jerusalem. A handful of Christian tourists become deluded each year and take on what they believe to be the voice, mannerisms, and attire of Jesus. Many wear nothing but a hotel bed sheet as they preach their message on Jerusalem's sidewalks.

Psychologists call this extreme form of Christlikeness "the Jerusalem syndrome." Not surprisingly, the turn of the millennium saw an increase in the number of people it affected. As many as 50 a week needed hospitalization from the disorder. Fortunately, counselors typically help victims overcome their delusion after a week of therapy.

Or consider the practice of reenacting Jesus' crucifixion each year in the Philippines. Young men choose actual beatings, carrying of a cross, and nails driven into their wrists. They even choose death in their desire to imitate Jesus and the events surrounding His sacrifice. Unfortunately, strong forces in the Philippine religious culture encourage this suicidal custom.

These strange syndromes remind us that we must be

more specific when we urge others to be Christlike. Imitation is not about wearing tunics, adopting Jesus' language, or reenacting His suffering and crucifixion. Being Christlike actually means living a life of love.

Jesus is our love model. He is not a mad scientist intent on making clones of himself. We imitate God when we imitate Jesus, and this means living lives of love. Christlikeness is love in action.

Set Apart   SEPARATION

We saw earlier that the idea of being set apart is a contributory notion of holiness. Now we see that being set apart is best understood as having to do with love. Those who choose a life of love distinguish themselves as a community that seeks to promote well-being.

Being part of this distinguished community is not a matter of exclusion or isolationism. Instead, communal love embraces others. The main difference between the community of the holy and other communities is the lifestyle of love that characterizes Holiness people. It is a peculiar people who love persistently.

Being set apart as an expression of holiness is also manifest in God's specific calls to love in particular ways at particular times. A specific call is the first step in being set apart. But this divine call requires our response.

This helps us make sense of biblical passages that refer to God's sanctifying us and our sanctifying ourselves. Setting apart involves both God's call and our response. We are holy when we respond to that call and work cooperatively with God to promote the well-being of others and of all creation, including ourselves. For God calls everyone to the work of love.

To follow God's command to "be holy, for I am holy" does not mean that we become all-knowing, omnipresent, or almighty. Instead, to be holy as God is holy means that we love as God loves. While we are different from God in so many ways, we can be like God when we respond to God's wooing. We imitate God as we live in love. We are sanctified, separate, and/or set apart when we love as God loves. And this setting apart involves both God's initiating action and our cooperative response.

Perfection

The final contributory notion of holiness we examined in chapter two has to do with perfection. Holiness as perfection is understandable when perfection is characterized as living in love. John Wesley called it "perfect love."

Two notions of holiness as perfect love are useful. The first comes from Aristotle's view that someone or something was perfect if it fulfilled its purpose. In terms of holiness, Aristotelian perfection means fulfilling our purpose to live lives of love. We are perfect when we act as the lovers God intended us to be.

The second notion of perfection may be even more important for what it implies for holiness. We can be perfect in any particular moment when we respond appropriately in that moment to God's call. This is holiness as perfection in each instant.

Holiness as moment-by-moment perfection begins as God makes a decision about how to love all creatures in a particular moment of time. Because God is perfect, we can rest assured that divine love is perfectly expressed in every moment, everlastingly.

Each instance of divine love includes a call for us to love. We are perfect if we respond appropriately to God's call to love in that particular moment. When we love in a given instant, we imitate God by being perfect as God is perfect. Christians *can* be perfect—in this sense!

Many Holiness theologians in recent centuries have claimed that it is possible to overcome sin in this life. Our suggestion that we can be perfect in any particular moment when we respond in love to God's call of love offers a realistic way to affirm this claim. After all, when we love as God calls, we do not sin. Because of God's enabling in each moment of our lives, sin is not inevitable. Love is always possible.

Moment-by-moment decisions to love, when strung together in a series, produce a lifestyle of righteousness. Repeated proper responses generate habits of love, and habits of love form a loving character. Saints are those who develop a lifestyle of love, and they stand as poignant witnesses to grace at work in the world. These virtuous ones also enjoy the benefits of abundant life that love brings.

In sum, the contributory notions of holiness we explored in chapter two, when rightly understood and when used appropriately, are expressions of the core of holiness —love. So long as we understand them as expressions of holiness and not its essence, they can help us understand better what it means to promote well-being.

Holiness as love promotes abundant life. We enhance the common good when we act holy, because we encourage peace, harmony, and the transformation of the individual, the community, and society. The adventure of relational holiness makes God's world a better place. And it gives us a taste of what existence beyond this life will be like.

THE DANCE OF HOLINESS

The old pop song is correct: What the world needs now is love. We need to be holy—we need to love—today as much as ever. We need to love God with all our heart, with all our soul, and with all our mind. And we need to love our neighbor as ourselves (Matt. 22:37-39). Holiness as love is the foundation of God's good news.

When we love, each of us and the Holiness Movement in general can avoid going the way of the Myanmar pygmies. A movement that practices and understands love as its core will thrive rather than go extinct. The Holiness Movement will not die if its members respond in love to the God who loves us all.

One way to appreciate love as the heart of relational holiness is to compare holiness to dancing. This may seem like a strangely unexpected metaphor for a couple of Nazarene theologians to employ, but it has been suggested that "dinosaurs died because they couldn't dance." How might we keep Holiness teaching from a similar fate? Our suggestion is that we think of both God and ourselves as partners in the dance of life. For our comparison, let's call God the "Master Dancer."

Some might think that holiness entails that each of us dance alone on the dance floor while God rests somewhere at a distance. In this way of understanding, holiness as dance, we pretty much do our own thing. We take no cues from God, or from anyone else for that matter. We prance around on our own in resolute determination to do the right thing. We might call this the "do my own thing dance."

It takes no time at all for this dance to turn into a fiasco. Chaos reigns when dancers do not follow an expert's lead, design, or plan. Participants thrash around, smash into each other, and cause injury and havoc. This is not poetry in motion. It is the mosh pit of despair. While dancers might occasionally glance at the Master Dancer, each is not the least concerned to follow directions. The extreme individualism of the "do my own thing dance" has little in common with relational holiness.

Another way to think of the holiness dance is to believe it prescripted and controlled. In it, the Master Dancer approaches us and says, "You *must* dance with Me. You *must* dance in the way that I command." When the dance is sovereignly restricted, we spin about like robots. Obedience is demanded, and variation is not tolerated. Let's call this the "divine coercion dance."

In contrast to the chaos of the "do my own thing dance," the "divine coercion dance" is utterly orderly. It is hard to imagine, though, that either the Master Dancer or the others participating actually appreciate and value each other. After all, robots don't love. And manipulators have no capacity for the risk that love requires.

In the "divine coercion dance" we find no good reason to regard the Master Dancer's request and subsequent leading as expressions of love. This exercise lacks freedom, adventure, and creative expression. While not ugly, it is eminently regimented and determinately dull.

The third way to think about holiness as a dance—and the way of relational holiness—is to think of the Master Dancer as acting first to request our hands. We retain the freedom to accept or reject that request. Should we reject it, the Master Dancer will continue to propose that we join Him. He never tires of requesting our hands. And if we accept, we begin to twirl cooperatively around the floor. Let's call this the "cooperation dance."

In the "cooperation dance," the Master Dancer takes the lead. Naturally when we follow the guidance of an expert, what ensues is beautiful poetry in motion. When we keep in step with the Master Dancer, the floor comes alive. We see the beauty of holiness.

The "cooperation dance" begins in beauty, but it can become even more exquisite as it grows more complex. The Master Dancer starts with the basic steps and proceeds to teach willing partners more and more intricate maneuvers. There seems no end to the delightful variations and adaptations that emerge as dancers collaborate.

After we've said "yes" to the request, however, we may get out on the dance floor and flop around sloppily. We can ignore the Master Dancer's charming moves, gentle nudging, and tender leadership. We can freely choose to get out of step with the Expert. The dance that once was beautiful becomes unsightly. Charm and creativity exit as the dance disintegrates into the "do my own thing dance."

The "cooperation dance" is not merely about our own response to the promptings of the Master Dancer. After all, He requests dances with everyone, and He aims to lead all who respond on the dance floor.

The "cooperation dance" also emphasizes that dancers can learn from other dancers as all follow the lead of the Master. In fact, dancers exchange advice. Throughout the dance's long history, participants have discovered steps and maneuvers that produce beautiful results. The Master Dancer seems often to lead dancers with these moves. Of course, beautiful dancing is ultimately about responding to the Master Dancer and secondarily about following proven techniques. But the techniques regularly serve as main means to the enriching ends that all dancers seek.

Dancing cooperatively with the Master changes, little by little, the dancers themselves. The relations that dancers have with the Master and each other literally change them into different persons. In fact, rather than only dancing beautifully, those who follow the Master's lead become beautiful dancers. This subtle difference in description identifies the importance of both *acting* as dancers and *being* dancers. Both acting and being require responding to the step-by-step, moment-by-moment guidance of the Master. Acting and being mesh.

In sum, the dance of holiness is a cooperative dance of

love. God acts first, we respond, and along with others who also respond appropriately to God, we set out on an adventure to make our world a more beautiful place—maybe even the kind of place God can call "very good" (Gen. 1:31).

And to this we say, "Let the dance begin!"

Questions to Stimulate Discussion

1. Why ought those who identify with the Holiness tradition regard love as the core of holiness?

2. The contributory notions of holiness are shown in this chapter to be potential expressions of love. Which explanation of the contributory notions did you find most helpful? Why?

3. Christians can act perfectly, according to the authors. What do they mean by this? How is this possible?

4. What do you find the most helpful point of the holiness-as-dancing analogy?

5. How are *acting as* dancers and *being* dancers related?

6. What hope do you have that the Holiness tradition can expand rather than go extinct as it emphasizes love as its core notion?

7. What is the most important insight you received from this book?

FOR DEEPER STUDY

Ackerman, David. "The Crisis of the Cross." In *Generation Xers Talk About the Church of the Nazarene*. Edited by Thomas Jay Oord. Kansas City: Beacon Hill Press of Kansas City, 1999.

Bond, Jim L. "The Most Beautiful Thing in the World." In *Holiness 101: Exploring This Transforming Journey*. Kansas City: Beacon Hill Press of Kansas City, 2003.

Butler, Christi. "Feminism and Life." In *Generation Xers Talk About the Church of the Nazarene*. Edited by Thomas Jay Oord. Kansas City: Beacon Hill Press of Kansas City, 1999.

Cartwright, Michael. "The Once and Future Church Revisited." In *Embodied Holiness: Toward a Corporate Theology of Spiritual Growth*. Edited by Samuel M. Powell and Michael E. Lodahl. Downers Grove, Ill.: InterVarsity Press, 1999.

Carver, Frank G. "Growth in Sanctification: John Wesley and John of the Cross." *The Tower: The Journal of Nazarene Theological Seminary* 3 (1999).

Daniels, T. Scott. "Generation X and Iconography: A Generation's Need for Narrative Worship." In *Generation Xers Talk About the Church of the Nazarene*. Edited by Thomas Jay Oord. Kansas City: Beacon Hill Press of Kansas City, 1999.

Dunning, H. Ray. *A Layman's Guide to Sanctification*. Kansas City: Beacon Hill Press of Kansas City, 1991.

Hamner, Philip R. "Entire Sanctification: No Apologies." In *Holiness 101: Exploring This Transforming Journey*. Kansas City: Beacon Hill Press of Kansas City, 2003.

Holiness 101: Exploring This Transforming Journey. Kansas City: Beacon Hill Press of Kansas City, 2003.

Hoskins, Steven T. "Longing for Home." In *Generation Xers Talk About the Church of the Nazarene*. Edited by Thomas Jay Oord. Kansas City: Beacon Hill Press of Kansas City, 1999.

Keen, Craig. "The Human Person as Intercessory Prayer." In *Embodied Holiness: Toward a Corporate Theology of Spiritual Growth*. Edited by Samuel M. Powell and Michael E. Lodahl. Downers Grove, Ill.: InterVarsity Press, 1999.

King, Thomas J. "Living the Holiness Lifestyle While in Exile." *Holiness Today*, May 1999.

Knight, Henry H. III. *A Future for Truth: Evangelical Theology in a Postmodern World*. Nashville: Abingdon Press, 1997.

Lanham, Jan Simonson. "To Serve the Present Age." In *Holiness 101: Exploring This Transforming Journey*. Kansas City: Beacon Hill Press of Kansas City, 2003.

Leupp, Roderick. "Knowing the Holy God." *Holiness Today*, February 2004.

Lyons, George. *Holiness in Everyday Life*. Kansas City: Beacon Hill Press of Kansas City, 1992.

———. *More Holiness in Everyday Life*. Kansas City: Beacon Hill Press of Kansas City, 1997.

Maddox, Randy L. "A Change of Affections: The Development, Dynamics, and Dethronement of John Wesley's 'Heart Religion.'" In *"Heart Religion" in the Methodist Tradition and Related Movements*. Edited by Richard Steele. Metuchen, N.J.: Scarecrow Press, 2001.

Moore, Frank. *Coffee Shop Theology: Translating Doctrinal Jargon into Everyday Life*. Kansas City: Beacon Hill Press of Kansas City, 1998.

Oord, Thomas Jay. "Evil, Providence, and a Relational God." *Quarterly Review* 23:3 (fall 2003).

Pearson, Karen, and Tim Milburn. "The Culture of Interactive Holiness." In *Holiness 101: Exploring This Transforming Journey*. Kansas City: Beacon Hill Press of Kansas City, 2003.

Preusch, Dana. "Commitment and Generation X." In *Generation Xers Talk About the Church of the Nazarene*. Kansas City: Beacon Hill Press of Kansas City, 1999.

Purkiser, W. T. "Holiness as Love of God." In *Biblical Resources for Holiness Preaching: From Text to Sermon*. Vol. 1, edited by H. Ray Dunning and Neil B. Wiseman. Kansas City: Beacon Hill Press of Kansas City, 1993.

Reed, Gerard. *C. S. Lewis and the Bright Shadow of Holiness*. Kansas City: Beacon Hill Press of Kansas City, 1999.

Rice, Richard. *The Openness of God*. Nashville: Review and Herald Publishing Association, 1980.

Spaulding, Henry W. II. "A Reconstruction of the Wesleyan Understanding of Christian Perfection." *Wesleyan Theological Journal* 33:2 (fall 1998).

Stanley, Susie C. *Holy Boldness: Women Preachers' Autobiographies and the Sanctified Self.* Knoxville, Tenn.: University of Tennessee Press, 2002.

Staples, Rob L. "Holiness as Christlikeness (Phil. 2:5-11)." In *Biblical Resources for Holiness Preaching: From Text to Sermon.* Vol. 2., edited by H. Ray Dunning. Kansas City: Beacon Hill Press of Kansas City, 1993.

Stiles, Kenton. "Religion and Aesthetics." In *Philosophy of Religion: Introductory Essays.* Edited by Thomas Jay Oord. Kansas City: Beacon Hill Press of Kansas City, 2003.

Stone, Bryan P. "Divine Presence." In *Philosophy of Religion: Introductory Essays.* Edited by Thomas Jay Oord. Kansas City: Beacon Hill Press of Kansas City, 2003.

Sunberg, Teanna. "Holiness: The Only Message of Hope." In *Holiness 101: Exploring This Transforming Journey.* Kansas City: Beacon Hill Press of Kansas City, 2003.

Swoope, Diana L. *Chosen and Highly Favored: A Woman's Sacred Call to Holiness.* Kansas City: Beacon Hill Press of Kansas City, 2001.

Wetmore, Gordon. "The Ministry of the Holy Spirit." *Proclaiming the Spirit.* Edited by Harold Bonner. Kansas City: Beacon Hill Press of Kansas City, 1975.